The Tess Mallos

FILLO PASTRY
COOKBOOK
And Introducing Kataifi Pastry

PHOTOGRAPHS BY
ANDREW WARN

ILLUSTRATIONS BY
SUZANNE MALLOS

MEREHURST PRESS
LONDON

*To my husband John, who married me in the hope that one day I would learn
to cook his favourite sweet, Baklava.*

Published 1987 by Merehurst Press
5 Great James Street
London WC1N 3DA

By arrangement with Reed Books Pty Ltd
2 Aquatic Drive Frenchs Forest NSW 2086

© Tess Mallos 1983

ISBN 0 948075 47 3

Photography by Andrew Warn
Designed by Warren Penney

Printed and bound by Dai Nippon Printing Co (Hong Kong) Ltd

CONTENTS

INTRODUCTION 5

ALL ABOUT FILLO PASTRY 6

Background to Fillo Pastry, Buying and Storing Fillo Pastry, Fillo Statistics, Fillo Without Tears, Home-Made Fillo Pastry, Freezer Storage of Prepared Pastries

LITTLE WRAP-UPS 13

BIGGER WRAP-UPS 27

THE BIG WRAP 51

PIES AND TARTS 69

KATAIFI 83

USING THE RECIPES 94

Measures and Oven Temperatures, Glossary of Ingredients

ACKNOWLEDGEMENTS

I am always grateful to those who assist me when putting together a cookbook. Thanking them is the very least I can do.

Naturally the manufacturers of fillo pastry played a most important part. Besides their endeavours which, in making fillo pastry widely available in Australia, have made this book possible, they gave freely both of their time (to answer my many queries) and their products (for testing and photography). I am grateful to Harry Larcos, Jim and Andrew Koumi and Robert Polycarpou of Athens Fine Pastry Pty Ltd, and to Chris Antoniou and his son Tony, of C. & M. Antoniou. Breakfast Kataifi (page 84) is Chris Antoniou's special contribution.

Fillo pastry is not of much use unless you have something to wrap it around. Thank you to the Australian Meat and Live-stock Corporation for supplying meat for testing and photography; to Cheryl Goodman and her team at the New South Wales Fish Marketing Authority for supplying information and seafoods; and to John Miller of the Australian Mushroom Growers Association for the edible fungi — much appreciated (and relished).

Norma Hickson was my patient and very able typist, and as she is a recent graduate in Home Science, assisted me with some of the testing and food preparation for photography.

Working with Diane Furness, my editor, has been a delight. Her dedication and attention to detail are much appreciated, as too, is the work of the designer, Warren Penney.

Having a daughter who was drawing from the time she could put pencil to paper, it was only a matter of time before I could make use of her talents. At last I have done so. Besides having to thank her for not defacing any walls during her formative years, I cannot help but be proud of her efforts in preparing the illustrations so necessary in a book of this nature. Sue also ably assisted me with the food preparation for photography — she can cook too!

A very special thank you to photographer Andrew Warn for his excellent work and for allowing me to have my way — sometimes.

Last but not least, my husband John, whose patience, understanding and contributions too numerous to mention made my task in getting it all together just that much less difficult.

INTRODUCTION

There was a time when the skill of a cook was measured by the lightness and succulence of her pastry. The industrial age of cookery, with factory-made foods to lighten the burden of the home cook, has almost eliminated pastry-making from the cook's repertoire. Packaged mixes which need a simple blending in of water, pastries made up ready to roll out or rolled ready for use, fill our pantries, freezers and refrigerators.

While it has been available to the cook for many years, fillo, the tissue-thin Greek pastry (pronounced fill-o), is more recently becoming the most popular pastry, particularly as a substitute for puff pastry. But its place in today's lifestyle makes fillo a pastry which can be used to great advantage as you can prepare many foods ahead and refrigerate or freeze them until required for cooking and serving. A more important plus for fillo is that you can control the amount of fat (butter or oil for example) in the finished pastry.

Since the publication of my books on Greek and Middle Eastern cooking, I have often given cooking demonstrations on these cuisines. Invariably I have found my audience engrossed when I have used fillo (and intrigued by kataifi pastry). Through feed-back, it seems most cooks have wanted to try their hand at cooking with fillo — only to end up in despair, with sheets sticking together or crumbling to pieces. In fact it seems likely that the excellence of a cook might soon be judged by the ability to handle fillo pastry!

So the idea was born to produce a book on the ins-and-outs of fillo. This is not a book you will use every day, but it will prove invaluable for special occasions. If the experience of a colleague is any guide, you could recoup half the book's cost with the first dish you attempt. (She went through four packages for one dish; the wrapper failed to tell her to leave the pastry at room temperature before attempting to open out the sheets.)

To present the complete fillo story, I have left little uncovered. In the following pages I shall describe what it is, how it is made, how to buy, handle, store, cut, wrap and cook it; as well as giving details on buttering, butter substitutes and oil and how to get them on to the fillo in the quickest possible way.

Kataifi occupies only a small part of this book. I have included it as many cooks are becoming aware of its availability. This pastry is also made by the producers of fillo pastry, so there is the connection.

Fillo is spelt in many different ways in publications — *filo, fillou, phyllo, phylo* and so on. The word *fillo* comes from the Greek word meaning 'leaf'. *Filo* is the Greek word for 'friend'. With transliterations (where words are represented in more or less corresponding characters of a different language), it is better to use a phonetic transliteration rather than to try to give letters which approximate the original language. The 'f' and 'i' of Greek are transliterated as 'ph' and alternate between 'y' and 'i' in scientific words — so let us leave the prerogative to the scientists; the makers of fillo and I prefer simplicity — spell it as you say it! After all there are moves towards phonetic spelling — or should that be fonetik!

Tess Mallos

ALL ABOUT FILLO PASTRY

BACKGROUND
TO FILLO PASTRY

While the origin of fillo is lost in the mists of time, it has been generally regarded as a Greek pastry. No doubt its recognition as such in Western countries could be attributed to the enterprising Greek immigrants who first began to make it for their compatriots, and gradually introduced it to their adopted country.

Fillo pastry, until relatively recently, was made by hand, though in some smaller cities you can still find exponents of the art. For an art it is. A ball of dough is expertly tossed and whirled on the backs of the hands to open it out, and as the circle becomes larger, it is tossed and whirled on the bent arm and shoulder until the sheet almost reaches the floor. It is then flipped out onto an 8-foot square table and stretched to tissue paper thinness, completely covering the table top. A heated blanket is spread on top to dry the pastry out a little. As each sheet is opened out it is finished on the same table and covered with a heated blanket. The edges of the pastry are then trimmed and the sheets cut to size, stacked, folded and wrapped.

Today major manufacturers of fillo pastry use machines which were originally designed in Vienna for strudel pastry, and adapted by Dutch and American engineers for making fillo. A machine can produce 100 kilograms (220 pounds) of fillo in an hour, about 60 kilograms (130 pounds) more than the amount two experts could make in a day by hand.

No doubt there are those who might claim fillo pastry is not of Greek origin. While this is arguable, there is one small clue which might shed some light.

Baklava is probably the best known of all the fillo pastry sweets. The name itself, as with a number of names of Greek recipes, is similar to the Turkish, Arabic and Iranian names of a similar pastry. The Greek version of Baklava contains walnuts or a mixture of walnuts and almonds, with the cooked pastry bathed in a honey-flavoured syrup. In the last chapter of Homer's *Odyssey*, there is a reference to 'psomi karathoglyko', meaning 'bread and walnut sweet'. As the bread of Ancient Greece (and Rome) was frequently referred to as 'pastry', and as honey was the sweetener of the day, it is quite probable that Homer wrote of an early version of Baklava. The *Odyssey* was written around 800 B.C.

BUYING AND STORING FILLO PASTRY

The invention of machines to make fillo has vastly improved the marketing of the pastry. Today, sheets can be cut to size, stacked and enclosed in plastic film and packaged attractively. Some makers prefer to sell only the chilled product, while others provide both the chilled and frozen product. The fillo has a long storage life; even when stored in the refrigerator it will keep for about 3 months, and it can be stored even longer in the freezer.

Where hand-made fillo is the only type available, it may be frozen if long-term storage is required, though it will keep for at least 2 weeks in the refrigerator, properly wrapped.

Chilled Fillo

If bought chilled, then simply store in the refrigerator. If you have had trouble with a particular brand previously, it is wise to check the sealed plastic bag in the carton. If there is a hole in the seal (machines are not always perfect), then leave the package at room temperature for 1-2 hours, open and check if fillo leaves are still pliable or dried out and brittle. If the latter, then return package to the store as refrigeration has a drying effect on the sheets.

Frozen Fillo

While conditions during cartage to the retailer can be controlled to a certain degree by the manufacturer or distributor, once the frozen fillo is on sale, the responsibility lies with the purchaser. With any frozen foods, it is wise to take an insulated container or bag with you to the supermarket so that frozen foods may be placed directly into it from the freezer cabinet. It is particularly important for fillo pastry as it can be well on the way to thawing as you line up at the check-out, and thaw even more on the way home. For further details, see Handling Frozen Fillo (page 8).

FILLO STATISTICS

Unfortunately, fillo manufacturers differ in determining the size and number of sheets in packs of the same weight. The thickness of the sheets also varies. Commercially packaged fillo, fresh or frozen, can vary in length from 40-50 cm (16-20 inches); the width is usually the same — about 30 cm (12 inches). There are slight variations between packs from the same manufacturer as the fillo is cut by hand — too delicate a job to be entrusted to machinery.

The number of sheets in a 375 g (12 oz) pack varies. Where sheets are longer, there are about 24-25 sheets to a pack as opposed to 28-30 sheets of the shorter fillo. A 500 g (1 lb) pack (often hand-made fillo) contains 32-35 sheets.

Basic shaping and wrapping instructions, and recipes, often give two measurements to indicate size. Once you have begun working with fillo, you will know which size to follow. To clarify instructions for the folding of fillo sheets in many of the recipes, see illustrations (page 12).

FILLO WITHOUT TEARS

Read that as you will, but the principal reason for this book is to eliminate the frustration cooks have experienced when handling the product. The following is your kitchen manual on fillo pastry; it answers all those queries you might have had, and more.

One of the first questions people ask when they begin to work with fillo is 'what should it be like?' Firstly, the sheets should be easy to separate singly. You can tell if a fillo is of top quality if you can crumple a sheet in your hand then spread it out again. Sometimes, with extended storage, this quality is diminished although the sheets are still usable.

Working with Fillo

Remove the pack from refrigerator and leave unopened at room temperature for 2 hours before attempting to open out sheets. Fillo straight from the refrigerator is stiff and if opened out too soon, could break at the folds. Spread a dry tea towel on a flat surface and place fillo on top. Cover with a thick cloth (2 tea towels or a large folded tea towel, so long as fillo is entirely covered). Wet another cloth, wring out well and place on top of stack. This way any air that filters through to the fillo is slightly moist.

Avoid working in very hot, dry conditions, and avoid draughts, fans and strong air conditioning. A humid atmosphere or cool kitchen helps with the handling of fillo.

Handling Fillo

Frozen fillo Success with frozen fillo pastry begins with its purchase. Take an insulated container or bag to the market, preferably with a frozen ice pack in it. Place fillo directly in this from the freezer cabinet. Failing this, wrap the package in plenty of newspaper — an excellent insulator. Place in the home freezer as soon as possible, and take care that warm food to be frozen is not placed on or near the frozen fillo; it is a good idea to store frozen fillo with other frozen foods closely packed around it.

Freeze-thaw cycles adversely affect fillo because of the condensation which forms on the pack; this in turn drips onto the fillo and softens the surface sheets. The frozen product is formulated to withstand a few of these cycles during the transition from manufacturer, through distribution points to the store freezer. It is up to the purchaser to ensure that no more freeze-thaw cycles occur until it is to be used.

To use frozen fillo, remove pack from freezer to refrigerator and leave to thaw slowly for 12 hours at least. Slow thawing eliminates condensation. When thawed, leave the pack at room temperature for 2 hours before attempting to open out sheets. While frozen fillo is convenient for many reasons, be prepared to lose the outer sheet or two.

Chilled fillo Remove pack from refrigerator 2 hours before required so that it comes to room temperature.

Hand-made fillo This should be stored in the refrigerator, adequately protected. If it is to be frozen, open out the stack of sheets and place a sheet of waxed paper on top. Fold up again and wrap closely in waxed paper, then plastic film. Overwrap with a plastic freezer bag and seal well with tape. Thaw as for Frozen Fillo and bring to room temperature.

To use hand-made fillo, open out sheets and brush off excess flour from each sheet. Re-stack sheets, then proceed with recipe.

Unused fillo Do not refreeze. Fold up sheets, return to plastic bag and seal with masking or freezer tape. Place in box, seal and store in refrigerator.

Fillo and the microwave oven Surprisingly you can thaw fillo in the microwave oven. No condensation occurs, but the fillo does dry out a little. Defrost on the DEFROST setting for 3 minutes, turning pack over each minute. Leave in its pack for 1 hour at room temperature before opening. Only use this method when time does not permit slow thawing. If the fillo does dry too much, see section on Resurrecting Fillo (page 9).

As far as cooking is concerned, it can only be done successfully if you have a microwave oven incorporating convection or gas heating. Cooking small pastries on the browning dish gives passable results, but only just. Reheating in a normal microwave oven causes the fillo to soften.

Cutting fillo Use a sharp, fine-bladed knife, sharp kitchen scissors or a Stanley knife (available at hardware stores). If a number of sheets have to be cut into strips, work with the number of required sheets placed in a stack on a large board and cut through the stack guiding the knife with a ruler. Stack and cover with dry and damp cloths.

Fillo Problems

Crumbling fillo Sheets that are stiff and break up easily are impossible to use so don't try. This condition is caused by fillo drying out. The package may not have been properly sealed during storage or the sheets not protected sufficiently while working with them.

Sheets sticking together This is caused by too much moisture. It can happen if condensation forms on the plastic enclosing the sheets, which then drops onto the pastry, softening it to the extent that the sheets stick together. To avoid condensation, slowly thaw frozen fillo in its pack in the body of the refrigerator. Also avoid placing a damp cloth in direct contact with fillo sheets while working with them.

Usually when fillo sticks together, only part of the stack of sheets might be affected. Cut off the offending section(s) and work with the remainder.

Resurrecting Fillo Pastry

When fillo is fairly stiff and crumbly around the edges, it is difficult or impossible to use. However with a little patience it is possible to revive the pastry sufficiently so that you may work with it.

Leave the pack at room temperature for 2 hours before attempting to open out the sheets. If it is difficult to open them out without breaking them at the folds, then the fillo is past help. However, if you can open out the sheets, continue in this manner. They probably will not lie flat, but this will improve during the treatment.

Place a damp cloth on a flat surface and cover with a dry cloth. Place opened fillo on top and cover completely with a dry cloth. Place a damp cloth on top of the stack and cover the top of this with a sheet of thick plastic. Leave for 20 minutes or until top sheets look slightly wrinkled. Remove plastic and top cloths. Turn a quarter of the fillo sheets over and place to one side. Turn the remaining fillo sheets upside down, lift up half of these sheets and turn these upside down onto stack still on cloths. Cover top with dry cloth, damp cloth and plastic and leave for another 20 minutes or so. The idea is to replace the dampened sheets amongst dry sheets, and these will in turn transfer moisture to the dry sheets. When the top sheets look slightly wrinkled check through the sheets to see if some sheets still look dry. Reposition them so that they come into contact with slightly damp sheets.

Try not to turn wrinkled sheets onto wrinkled sheets otherwise they will stick. When you see that most sheets look a little wrinkled, remove the cloths from the bottom and replace with a dry cloth. Stack fillo on top, place a dry cloth over stack and place an empty, large baking dish on top, base down. This will help flatten the sheets. After another 30 minutes remove dish and cloths, place fillo stack onto a board and using a long ruler as a guide, cut off the ragged edges. Fillo is then ready for use. As you work with the sheets keep the remainder covered with a doubled dry cloth topped with a slightly damp cloth.

Adding the Fat

For baked fillo, a fat (such as butter or oil) has to be applied to the sheets to give the characteristic lightness, crispness and puff. While butter or oil is used in recipes, there are alternatives. Butter gives consistently good results for most recipes because of its flavour and is recommended for sweet fillo dishes. Margarine may be used in place of butter, but use a good quality margarine for better flavour. To cut costs, a mixture of butter and margarine or a mixture of butter and oil may be used. Olive oil is excellent for some savoury dishes where its flavour is essential; however a good quality olive oil should be used.

Butter Salted or unsalted (sweet) butter may be used. However salted butter has a longer shelf life and is usually cheaper than unsalted. As the butter has to be melted, salted butter can be de-salted in the process. As it also contains milk solids, these have to be removed after melting. In other words the butter is clarified or drawn. If milk solids are brushed on to the fillo these darken during baking and show up as dark patches on the finished pastry.

Clarified or drawn butter: Place butter in a small pan and melt over low heat. Skim froth from the top; if using salted butter this froth contains the salt, effectively de-salting the butter. Let butter stand for a minute or so to allow the milk solids to settle. Pour or spoon off the oiled butter into a container, leaving milk solids in the pan. (Combine milk solids with froth and add to cooked vegetables.) Use clarified butter while warm.

Recipes simply refer to melted butter or substitute. The above is the butter referred to, while the following are the substitutes.

Butter substitutes These include ghee, clarified margarine, butter and oil combined and butter and margarine combined.

Ghee: An excellent substitute as it is pure butter fat. Just melt it.

Clarified margarine: Follow directions for clarifying butter, using a good quality margarine. With some margarines the froth is not as evident as with butter, and there is a fine scum on the surface rather than froth. As this is the salt, skim it off carefully if it is to be used in recipes for sweet pastries (fillo or kataifi). Let melted margarine stand for a few minutes then pour or spoon off the clear oil into a container, leaving liquid in pan.

Butter and oil: This combination is very good for flavour, lower cost, and balancing saturated and poly-unsaturated fats. For savoury foods you can use a combination of clarified butter and a bland cooking or salad oil — roughly equal parts of each. Warm butter and oil together.

Butter and margarine: Good for flavour and slightly less expensive. Put equal amounts of butter and margarine in a small pan, melt slowly and clarify as for clarified butter.

Oil Olive oil of good quality is recommended for some savoury pastries where the flavour enhances the dish being prepared. Low-grade olive oil or a mixture of olive and other oil can create an unpleasant flavour if the fillo dish is eaten cold. Peanut oil is recommended for Chinese-style recipes, though maize or a seed oil may be used.

Melted butter — a short cut This is how I usually handle melted butter when working with fillo. Slowly melt either butter or margarine, or a combination of the fats, in a small pan. Skim off froth. Apply straight from the pan without stirring with the brush. You will find that the liquid collects in the bottom of the pan, but by the time you get that far, the job is usually completed. Oil can be added to the melted butter — they will remain blended, while the liquid stays at the bottom of the pan.

Butter quantities Recipes do not give quantities except for traditional pastries which require a certain amount for the desired result, e.g. the various baklavas. Quantities are given for kataifi as this pastry does not absorb butter, and too much is wasteful.

Therefore, where recipes state melted butter or substitute, melt (and clarify) about ½ cup (125 g or 4 oz). If any is left over, store in a covered container in refrigerator for later use, or use it for other cooking. If you run short, it does not take long to melt more in the same pan.

Oil quantities are not given either. Pour a small amount, about ¼ cup, into a small bowl, adding more as required.

There is no need to be heavy handed when brushing on the fat used — a light coating is all that is required. **Too much butter on top of pastries will prevent browning.**

Using less fat This is the advantage fillo has over other pastries in that as good a result can be achieved with a little fat as with a lot. I have used as little as ¼ cup (60 g or 2 oz) for 250 g (8 oz) fillo — this is a quarter less fat than that which would be contained in an equivalent amount of puff pastry, and half of the fat used in a short crust. When you are counting calories and still like to enjoy an occasional pastry dish, fillo is definitely the answer, so long as fried and sweet pastries are avoided.

The brush Use a pure bristled pastry brush. For small pastries a brush 2.5 cm (1 inch) wide and 5 mm (¼ inch) thick is just right. The same brush may be used for larger pastries, but when brushing many layers of fillo for pies etc., a brush 3-4 cm (1¼-1½ inches) wide and about 1 cm (½ inch) thick does the job more efficiently. Do not use too large a brush as the bristles take in too much fat.

Cookware and Fillo

The most frequently used item of cookware for fillo pastry is the baking sheet (baking tray, biscuit tray, oven slide, call it what you will). As it is flat with edges slightly turned up, oven heat can circulate more freely around the pastries for even cooking and browning. Use baking sheets which conduct heat well and remain rigid in the oven. Thin baking sheets sometimes buckle with the oven heat, causing food to slide out of place.

Where a recipe calls for a baking dish, most types are suitable — aluminium, stainless steel, enamelled cast iron — or you may use ceramic or glass ovenproof dishes which can go from the oven to the table. Avoid tin and uncoated cast iron baking dishes if syrup is to be poured onto hot sweet pastries. These metals react with the sugar and discolour the syrup and the base of the pastries.

FREEZER STORAGE OF PREPARED PASTRIES

Because they take time to prepare, small fillo pastries may be assembled ahead and stored in the freezer. They must be frozen in the uncooked state as cooked fillo is very fragile. For pastries which are to be baked, place the finished pastries on a baking sheet covered with opaque freezer plastic film or foil. Brush tops of pastries with butter and cover with a sheet of freezer film. Place in freezer just long enough to freeze pastries solid then lift off carefully and pack into a rigid container, interleaving layers with film. Seal, label and store in freezer.

Pastries which are to be fried should be left on a cloth-lined tray until all pastries are shaped. Lift onto a baking sheet lined with freezer film or foil and brush tops and sides of pastries with cooking oil. Cover with freezer film or foil and freeze until firm, then pack into a rigid container, interleaving layers with freezer film. Seal, label and store in freezer. Keep no longer than 2 months.

To Cook Pastries from the Freezer

Baked pastries Place frozen pastries on greased baking sheets and cook from frozen state, allowing an extra 5 minutes baking time. Pastries may be brought to room temperature before baking if desired.

Fried pastries Place frozen pastries on a cloth-lined tray, cover with a cloth and leave to thaw (about 1 hour). Deep fry as for freshly made pastries, according to recipe.

HOME-MADE FILLO PASTRY

This is a recipe for the adventurous or those who do not have fillo available in their area. Equipment required: mixing bowl, rolling pin, wooden dowel no less than 60 cm (24 inches) long and 2 cm (¾ inch) in diameter, large work surface, large cloth and waxed paper.

4 cups plain white flour (bread flour)
1 teaspoon salt
1⅓ cups tepid water

¼ cup oil
(olive, maize or polyunsaturated)

Sift flour and salt into mixing bowl. Make a well in the centre and add water and oil. Gradually stir flour into liquid to form a soft dough, then knead in bowl with hand for 10 minutes — same as for bread dough. Dough is sticky to begin with, but becomes smooth and satiny as gluten is developed. Cover and let dough rest for 1 hour.

Divide pastry into 12 portions, shaping each into a smooth ball. Wrap each ball in plastic film.

Dust work surface lightly with sifted flour. Take a ball of pastry and shape it into a square. Place on work surface and dust top with flour. Roll out to a 15 cm (6 inch) square using rolling pin. Dust again with flour. Take dowel and place on one end of pastry. Roll pastry neatly onto dowel, pressing firmly as you roll. Keep hands on dowel at each side of pastry. Unroll pastry and dust work surface and pastry top again with flour. Roll up again from opposite side of pastry, again exerting pressure. Unroll carefully. After second rolling, pastry should be about 25 × 30 cm (10 × 12 inches) in size.

Using backs of hands (rings removed and with short finger nails), place hands under dough and stretch gently, moving hands to stretch it evenly, working towards edge. Work around the edges of the pastry giving them a final stretch with finger tips. You will end up with a piece of fillo about 36 × 46 cm (14 × 18 inches) in size. Place on a cloth (such as a piece of old sheeting), cover with waxed paper and fold cloth over top.

Repeat using remaining pastry, laying each completed sheet on top of previous one with waxed paper in between and replacing cloth cover. Trim edges of sheets with scissors and use soon after making as directed in recipes; for pies and layered pastries where a number of sheets are required, use half the number of home-made fillo sheets to those given in recipes. For baked small pastries, parcels, rolls etc. calling for folded fillo, adjust to reduce layers by half.

Do not be concerned if the pastry tears during stretching — they may be mended as fillo is being used by pressing torn edges together, or avoided if cutting into pieces or strips.

Note: The home-made fillo may be stored in the refrigerator for 3 days or so. Replace the waxed paper between the fillo sheets, fold into a long rectangle (as for commercially produced fillo), wrap in plastic film and overwrap with a plastic bag. Seal with tape and store. Bring to room temperature for 2 hours before opening out sheets.

These illustrations clarify the folding or cutting of fillo sheets in shaping directions and recipes:

Folding or cutting across length of pastry sheet.

Folding or cutting across width (or along length) of pastry sheet.

LITTLE WRAP-UPS

These little morsels launched fillo pastry into many a cook's repertoire. Cheese and Spinach Triangles and Boureks fired the imagination, inspired the cook and led to the pastry being used with an extensive range of fillings. Indian Samosa and Chinese Fried Wontons may also be made with fillo; it is a good substitute when wonton wrappers are unavailable in your area.

In keeping with the theme of the book, basic shaping of small pastries is covered in detail, including instructions for freezing, so necessary for today's lifestyle.

Once you have mastered the art of the little wrap-up, you can use other favourite fillings for the pastries. Remember to use cooled fillings when shaping as hot fillings soften the fillo making shaping difficult.

If serving pastries with different fillings, then make each type in a different shape to distinguish one from another.

As some small pastries are fried instead of baked, shaping instructions outline the preparation for each cooking method as they differ.

BASIC SHAPING

For small pastries the width of the pastry becomes the length of the strip, unless specific recipes state otherwise. 'Butter' refers to melted butter (see page 10) but can be a butter substitute (also detailed on page 10).

Preparing strips Stack the number of fillo sheets required on a flat surface. With a ruler or tape, measure the length of the pastry and divide evenly into width required for desired shape. Cut with a Stanley or other sharp knife against the ruler, or use kitchen scissors, cutting through the stack. Stack strips on a tray covered with a dry cloth, fold cloth over strips and place a damp cloth on top. Number of sheets required depends on length of fillo sheets, see Fillo Statistics (page 7).

Triangles

For baking Cut strips approximately 12 cm (5 inches) wide. Brush lightly with butter and fold strip in half lengthwise. Brush top with butter, place filling on end of strip and fold into triangles as illustrated. Place finished triangles on a lightly greased baking sheet and brush top lightly with butter.

For frying Cut strips approximately 6 cm (2½ inches) wide. Place filling on end of strip and fold up into a triangle. Brush end of strip lightly with water, complete fold and place fold side down on a cloth. Keep pastries covered with a dry cloth as they are prepared. As pastries for frying do not have the protection of butter, the pastry can dry out and flake.

Rolls

For baking Cut strips approximately 25 cm (10 inches) wide (or halve the sheet). Brush lightly with butter and fold strip in half lengthwise. Brush top with butter, place filling on end of strip 2 cm (¾ inch) in from base and sides. Fold base of pastry over filling and fold in sides. Roll up to end of strip (see illustration). Place join side down on a lightly greased baking sheet. Brush top lightly with butter.

For frying Cut strips approximately 12 cm (5 inches) wide. Place filling as for baking rolls. When sides are folded over filling, press folds along length of strip and brush them lightly with water. Roll up and lightly brush final flap with water to seal roll. Place join side down on a cloth-covered tray and cover with a dry cloth.

Using less fat When preparing pastries for baking, instead of buttering the entire width of the strip, lightly butter only half the width, then fold over. There is no way you can save on the fat if frying pastries, so avoid this method if you are counting calories.

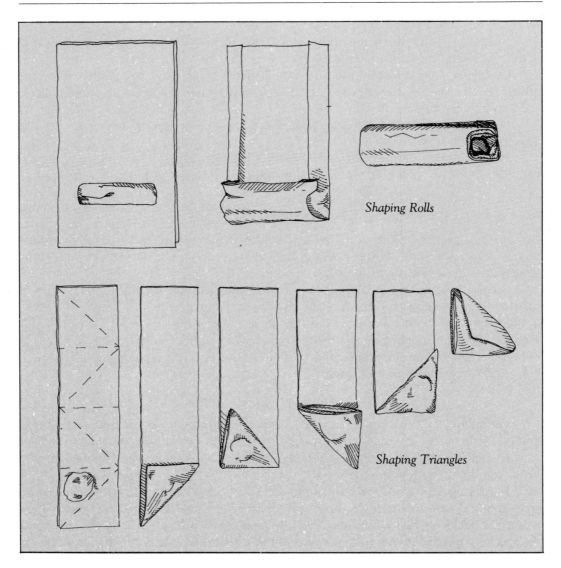

Shaping Rolls

Shaping Triangles

14

CHEESE TRIANGLES

Makes about 60 triangles or 48 rolls
Oven temperature
180-190°C (350-375°F)

CHEESE FILLING:
1 cup crumbled feta cheese
1 cup ricotta cheese
¼ cup finely chopped parsley
2 teaspoons finely chopped fresh mint
freshly ground black pepper
2-3 eggs, depending on size
TO FINISH:
12-18 sheets fillo pastry for Triangles
for Baking (page 13)
melted butter

Combine crumbled feta with ricotta cheese in a bowl then mash with a fork to blend thoroughly. Add parsley, mint and pepper to taste. Lightly beat eggs and stir into cheese.

The number of sheets required depends on their length. Cut fillo sheets, butter, fold, fill and shape as for Triangles for Baking directions, using a heaped teaspoon of filling for each triangle.

Place finished triangles on lightly greased baking sheet and brush tops lightly with butter. Bake in a moderately hot oven for 15 minutes or until puffed and golden. Serve hot.

Cheese Boureks Use ingredients as for above recipe. Cut pastry, butter, fold, fill and shape as directed for Rolls for Baking (page 14).

Use about a tablespoon of filling for each roll. Place join side down onto lightly greased baking sheets and brush rolls lightly with butter. Bake in a moderately hot oven for 20 minutes, until puffed and golden. Serve hot.
Note: These pastries freeze well. Follow instructions for Freezer Storage (page 11).

LITTLE SPINACH TRIANGLES

Makes about 48 triangles or 30 rolls
Oven temperature
180-190°C (350-375°F)

250 g (8 oz) packet frozen spinach,
thawed
1 cup chopped spring onions, including
some green tops
2 tablespoons butter
½ cup shredded Coon cheese or other
mature cheddar
¼ cup sour cream
1 tablespoon chopped parsley
pinch ground nutmeg
1 large egg
salt
freshly ground pepper
12-16 sheets fillo pastry for Triangles
for Baking (page 13)
melted butter

Use leaf or chopped spinach and drain well in a strainer, pressing out moisture with the back of a spoon. If leaf spinach, chop finely. Place in a bowl.

Gently fry spring onions in butter until just soft. Add to spinach with cheese, sour cream, parsley and nutmeg. Beat egg lightly and stir into spinach with salt and pepper to taste.

Cut fillo pastry into strips, butter, fold, fill and shape according to directions for Triangles for Baking, using a good teaspoon of filling for each triangle. Place join side down on greased baking sheets and brush tops lightly with butter. Bake in a pre-heated moderately hot oven for 20 minutes until puffed and golden. Serve hot.

Spinach Boureks Cut fillo sheets in half across their width, fold, fill and roll according to directions for Rolls for Baking (page 14), using 1 tablespoon filling for each roll. Place join side down on greased baking sheets and brush tops lightly with butter. Bake as for triangles.

Note: These freeze well. Follow directions for Freezer Storage of Pastries (page 11).

CORN PUFFS

Makes 56
Oven temperature
180-190°C (350-375°F)

PANADA (Thick White Sauce):
3 tablespoons butter
4 tablespoons flour
1 cup milk
salt
freshly ground pepper
TO FINISH:
300 g (10 oz) can creamed corn
1 egg yolk
14 sheets fillo pastry for Triangles
(page 13)
melted butter or substitute

A panada is a thick mixture for binding foods. For this and other recipes, the panada used is a thick white sauce.

Melt butter in a heavy pan, stir in flour and cook gently for 2 minutes until bubbling — do not let roux colour. Pour in milk, stirring constantly with a wooden spoon. If sauce lumps, remove from heat and stir well with a balloon whisk. Return to heat and stir until sauce is very thick and begins to boil. Boil on low heat for 2 minutes, remove from heat and turn into a bowl. Season to taste with salt and pepper.

Mix creamed corn into hot panada. When lukewarm mix in egg yolk. Adjust seasoning with salt and pepper and leave until cold.

Cut fillo into strips as directed for shaping Triangles for Baking. Butter and fold, butter top of strip and fill as directed using a heaped teaspoon of filling. Place join side down on greased baking sheet and brush tops with butter. Bake in a moderately hot oven for 12 minutes until puffed and golden.

BRAIN TRICORNS

Makes 48
Oven temperature
180-190°C (350-375°F)

2 sets lamb brains or 1 set calf brains
water
salt
1 small onion, quartered
small piece celery
½ bay leaf
¼ teaspoon whole peppercorns
2 teaspoons lemon juice or vinegar
1 quantity Panada (see
Corn Puffs page 16)
pinch ground nutmeg
1 egg yolk
12 sheets fillo pastry
melted butter or substitute

Soak lamb brains in salted water for 30 minutes to remove excess blood. If possible remove skin from brains (not possible if brains have been frozen). Return to salted water for another 15 minutes after skinning. Drain, rinse and place in a pan with onion, carrot, celery, bay leaf, peppercorns, lemon juice and about ½ teaspoon salt. Cover with cold water and bring to a slow simmer. Simmer gently, covered, for 15 minutes and leave in liquid to cool. Drain and dry brains, pull off loose skin and remove any veins. Cut into small dice.

Make a panada sauce as directed and, while hot, gently mix in diced brains. Cover surface with plastic film and when cooled to lukewarm, mix in egg yolk. Leave until cold.

Cut pastry into strips as directed for shaping Triangles for Baking (page 13) and brush with butter, fold and fill, using a heaped teaspoon of filling.

Shape into triangles. Place on greased baking sheet and brush tops lightly with butter. Bake in a moderately hot oven for 12 minutes.

Clockwise: *Plum Sauce (page 22); Seafood Fillo Rolls (page 20); Little Spinach Triangles (page 15); Ladies Fingers (page 22); Cheese Straws (page 23) and Fried Camembert Triangles (page 24).*

SAMOSA WITH VEGETABLE FILLING

Makes about 30

2 medium-sized potatoes
½ cup fresh or frozen green peas
¾ cup water
salt
½ teaspoon sugar
2 tablespoons oil
1 large onion, finely chopped
2 cloves garlic, crushed
1 teaspoon grated fresh ginger
1 small carrot, grated
¼-½ teaspoon chili powder
½ teaspoon ground turmeric
freshly ground pepper
2 tablespoons chopped fresh coriander
or mint
1 teaspoon garam masala
1 tablespoon lemon juice
5 sheets fillo pastry for Triangles for
Frying (page 13)
oil for deep or shallow frying

Peel potatoes and cut into 1 cm (½ inch) dice. Place in a saucepan with the peas, water, ½ teaspoon salt and the sugar. Cover and simmer until potatoes are just tender. Remove lid, increase heat and let most of the moisture evaporate. Keep aside.

In a frying pan heat oil, add onion and cook gently until transparent. Add garlic, ginger, carrot, chili powder to taste, turmeric and pepper and cook for 2 minutes. Add cooked potatoes and peas and any remaining liquid and cook on medium heat, stirring occasionally, until moisture evaporates. Stir in coriander or mint, garam masala and lemon juice, adjust flavour with salt, pepper and chili powder and remove from heat. Leave until cool.

Fill, shape and fry samosa as directed for Samosa with Meat Filling (page 19) and serve with Yoghurt Sauce (page 20).

Fried Wontons (page 21) and Chinese Chicken and Ham Rolls and Chicken and Crab Rolls (page 37).

SAMOSA WITH MEAT FILLING

Makes about 50

1 large onion, finely chopped
1 tablespoon butter or oil
2 cloves garlic, crushed
2 teaspoons grated fresh ginger
¼-½ teaspoon chili powder
1 teaspoon ground coriander
½ teaspoon ground turmeric
500 g (1 lb) finely ground lean beef
or lamb
½ cup water
salt
freshly ground pepper
2 tablespoons chopped fresh coriander
or mint
1 teaspoon garam masala
1 tablespoon lemon juice
8 sheets fillo pastry for Triangles for
Frying (page 13)
oil for deep or shallow frying

In a frying pan, with lid to fit, cook onion gently in butter or oil until transparent. Add garlic, ginger, chili powder to taste, ground coriander and turmeric and cook for further minute. Increase heat, add ground meat and cook over high heat, stirring to break up lumps. When colour changes reduce heat, add water and salt and pepper to taste. Cover and simmer gently for 15 minutes. Add coriander or mint and garam masala and cook, uncovered, until most of liquid evaporates. Stir in lemon juice and leave aside to cool.

Cut fillo sheets into strips approximately 6 cm (2½ inches) wide, stack and cover. Place a generous teaspoonful of filling on base of strip and fold into a triangle. Lightly brush end of strip with water and complete triangle. Place join side down on a cloth. Repeat with remaining ingredients.

Heat oil for deep frying and fry 3 to 4 samosa at a time, turning to brown evenly. If shallow frying is preferred, put oil in a frying pan to a depth of 5 mm (¼ inch), heat and shallow-fry, 6 to 8 at a time, turning to brown evenly. Remove and drain on absorbent paper. Serve hot with chutney or Yoghurt Sauce (page 20).

19

CURRY PUFFS

Makes about 50
Oven temperature
190-200°C (375-400°F)

2 tablespoons oil or ghee
1 large onion, chopped
1 teaspoon grated fresh ginger
1 clove garlic, finely chopped
3 teaspoons curry powder
500 g (1 lb) finely ground beef
1 cup chopped, peeled tomatoes
1 large potato, peeled and diced
salt
½ teaspoon garam masala
12-16 sheets fillo pastry for Triangles
for Baking (page 13)
Yoghurt Sauce for serving (page 20)

Heat oil or ghee in a frying pan, add onion and fry gently until soft. Add ginger, garlic and curry powder and cook gently for 5 minutes. Increase heat and add ground beef. Stir over high heat to break up lumps and cook until colour changes. Reduce heat, add tomatoes, diced potato and salt to taste. Cover and simmer gently for 15-20 minutes until potato is soft. Add a little water during cooking if necessary. At end of cooking, mixture should have very little moisture. Stir in garam masala, cook for a minute or so, then leave until cool.

Cut fillo pastry into strips, butter, fold, fill and shape into triangles as directed for Triangles for Baking, using a heaped teaspoon of filling for each triangle. Place on greased baking sheets and bake in a preheated moderately hot oven for 12-15 minutes until puffed and golden. Serve hot as an appetiser, with Yoghurt Sauce as a dipping sauce.

YOGHURT SAUCE

Makes about 1¼ cups

1½ cups natural yoghurt
1 small green cucumber
salt
1 crushed clove garlic, optional
½ teaspoon dried mint flakes

Place yoghurt in a doubled piece of butter muslin, gather up ends and tie with string. Suspend from a fixed object over a bowl and leave to drain for 1½ hours. Alternatively, drain yoghurt in a stainless steel, fine meshed sieve over a bowl. Grate cucumber and mix with 1 teaspoon salt (you will need about ¾ cup grated cucumber), place in a strainer and leave for 1 hour. Press with the back of a spoon to remove excess moisture.

Place drained yoghurt in a bowl, add drained cucumber, garlic if used and dried mint flakes rubbed to a powder. Mix well and add salt if necessary. Cover and chill until required and serve as a sauce or dip for pastries as directed in recipes.

SEAFOOD FILLO ROLLS

Makes 18 rolls

6 seafood or crab sticks
1 egg
1 tablespoon milk
¼ teaspoon Chinese five spice powder
¼ cup cornflour
3 sheets fillo pastry
oil for deep frying
FOR SERVING:
Chili Sauce (page 21) or
Plum Sauce (page 22)

Seafood or crab sticks are pressed seafood shaped into 12 cm (5 inch) sticks and are available frozen, though often sold thawed.

Thaw seafood sticks if necessary and cut each in 3 even pieces. Beat egg with milk and five spice powder. Dip seafood sticks into egg mixture and coat with cornflour.

Cut fillo sheets into 3 even pieces across the length of the sheets to give strips about 15-18 cm (6-7 inches) wide and 30 cm (12 inches) long, then cut in half so that pieces are almost square. Place a piece of seafood stick across one corner and in from sides. Fold corner of fillo over stick, fold in sides and brush folded sides and end flap of pastry lightly with water. Roll up firmly and place join side down onto absorbent paper. Shape remaining rolls.

Heat oil for deep frying and fry a few rolls at a time until crisp and golden brown, turning to brown evenly. Drain on absorbent paper and serve hot as an appetizer with Chili or Plum Sauce.

FRIED WONTONS

Makes about 50

250 g (8 oz) boneless pork
500 g (1 lb) green prawns
4 spring onions
1 teaspoon grated fresh ginger
1 tablespoon cornflour
2 teaspoons light soy sauce
½ teaspoon sugar
freshly ground black pepper
½ teaspoon salt
1 egg white
6-8 sheets fillo pastry, depending on size

Use pork fillet or meat cut from pork chops, including a little fat. Cube the meat. Shell prawns and devein, rinse and dry well with absorbent paper. Put pork, prawns and roughly chopped spring onions (including some green tops) in food processor bowl with steel blade fitted. Add ginger, cornflour, soy sauce, sugar, pepper to taste and salt. Process until a coarse paste is formed. Remove to bowl, cover and chill until needed.

Beat egg white lightly with a pinch of salt to help it break down. Take a sheet of fillo pastry and spread on a flat surface. Brush entire sheet evenly and lightly with egg white, keeping in a little from the edges. Place another sheet on top and smooth out as much as possible. Cut into approximately 10 cm (4 inch) squares with kitchen scissors. Stack and cover with a folded dry cloth. Repeat this process with another 4-6 sheets fillo — the number of sheets required depends on size of sheets.

Take a prepared square of pastry and place a teaspoon of the mixture in the centre and brush pastry edges lightly with egg white. Fold into a triangle and gently turn the right-angled point of the triangle up and bring the other two points together, dabbing one point lightly with a little egg white. Press one point on top of the other. (These are shaped like the Italian Tortellini.) Place finished wontons on a cloth and cover with another cloth.

To cook, deep fry in hot oil 3-4 at a time and cook for 2-3 minutes. Drain on absorbent paper and serve hot with Chili or Plum Sauce (pages 21 and 22) or the plum sauce available commercially. Wontons may be fried then reheated later in a moderate oven until crisp.
Note: These are not suitable for boiling as fillo pastry differs in composition to wonton wrappers. If such wrappers are available in your area, use these in place of the fillo sheets.

CHILI SAUCE

Makes about 1 cup

1 tablespoon oil
1 tablespoon grated fresh ginger
2 cloves garlic, crushed
¼ cup Chinese chili sauce
⅓ cup tomato sauce or ketchup
2 teaspoons light soy sauce
1 tablespoon dry sherry
¼ cup water
2 teaspoons brown sugar

Heat oil in a small saucepan, add ginger and garlic and cook gently for 1 minute. Add remaining ingredients and bring to the boil. Boil gently for 5 minutes until thick. Cool and store in a sealed jar in the refrigerator. It will keep for 2 weeks. Serve as a dipping sauce for Chinese fried pastries or as directed in recipes.

PLUM SAUCE

Makes 1 cup

¾ cup plum jam
⅓ cup white vinegar
¼ teaspoon ground ginger
¼ teaspoon ground allspice
⅛ teaspoon hot chili powder

Place all ingredients in a small pan and bring slowly to the boil, stirring often to melt jam. Boil gently for 2 minutes, remove from heat and cool. If jam has pieces of skin in it, you might prefer to puree the sauce in a blender. Pour into a clean bottle and store at room temperature. It will keep for some weeks. Serve as a dipping sauce for Chinese fried pastries or as directed in recipes.

LADIES' FINGERS

Makes about 36
Oven temperature
180-190°C (350-375°F)

2 tablespoons ghee or butter
½ cup pine nuts
1 large onion, finely chopped
500 g (1 lb) lean ground lamb
or young beef
¼ teaspoon ground cinnamon
salt
freshly ground black pepper
¼ cup chopped parsley
1 tablespoon chopped fresh mint
2 teaspoons lemon juice
18 sheets fillo pastry for Rolls
for Baking (page 14)
melted butter

Heat half the ghee in a frying pan, add pine nuts and fry over medium heat until golden, stirring often. Remove with a draining spoon to a plate.

To ghee left in pan, add onion and cook on gentle heat until transparent. Increase heat, add ground meat and cook, stirring often to break up lumps. When meat changes colour, reduce heat, add cinnamon, about 1 teaspoon salt and plenty of ground pepper. Cover and let meat simmer in its juices for 15 minutes. Remove lid and evaporate most of the juices. Stir in parsley, mint, lemon juice and browned pine nuts. Leave until cool.

Cut fillo sheets in half, butter, fold, fill and shape into rolls as directed, using a tablespoon filling for each roll. Place rolls on a lightly greased baking sheet and brush tops with butter. Bake in a moderately hot oven for 12-15 minutes until golden brown. Serve hot.

CRAB AND PECAN BITES

Makes about 30
Oven temperature
190-200°C (375-400°F)

1 tablespoon butter
1 cup chopped small mushrooms
1 teaspoon lemon juice
½ cup chopped celery
½ cup chopped pecans
170 g (5½ oz) can crab meat, drained
1 tablespoon chopped chives
1 tablespoon mayonnaise
1 tablespoon sour cream
salt
freshly ground pepper
8 sheets fillo pastry for Triangles
(page 13)
melted butter

Melt butter in a pan, add mushrooms, lemon juice and celery and fry gently for 5 minutes until moisture evaporates. Turn into a bowl and add pecans and chopped crab meat. Leave until cool then stir in chives, mayonnaise, sour cream and salt and pepper to taste.

Cut fillo into strips, butter, fold, fill and shape as directed for Triangles for Baking, using a generous teaspoon of filling for each. Place join side down onto greased baking sheet and bake in a moderately hot oven for 12-15 minutes until golden. Serve hot.

CHEESE STRAWS

Makes 24
Oven temperature
170-180°C (325-350°F)

½ cup grated parmesan cheese
¼ teaspoon cayenne pepper
12 sheets fillo pastry
melted butter
additional grated parmesan cheese

Mix cheese with cayenne. Butter 2 sheets fillo together, butter top and fold in half. Turn folded edge towards you. Brush again with butter and sprinkle evenly with 1 tablespoon of the cheese mixture, leaving 2 cm (¾ inch) of top edge clear. Roll up firmly into a roll. Cut evenly into four and place small rolls onto lightly greased baking sheet. Repeat with remaining ingredients. Brush tops of rolls with butter and sprinkle lightly with additional cheese. Bake in a moderate oven for 15-20 minutes until lightly browned and crisp. Cool on tray, pack into a container and seal. Serve with pre-dinner drinks. These will keep for 2 weeks — if necessary warm in a moderate oven for 5 minutes to freshen the flavour.

BACON AND ONION TRIANGLES

Makes 30
Oven temperature
180-190°C (350-375°F)

250 g (8 oz) bacon slices
2 medium-sized onions, finely chopped
1 tablespoon butter
½ cup soft breadcrumbs
freshly ground pepper
8 sheets fillo pastry for
Triangles for Baking (page 13)
melted butter or substitute

Remove rind from bacon if present. Chop bacon finely and place in a heated frying pan. Cook, stirring often, until fat renders and bacon is browned lightly. Add onion and cook gently until onion is transparent. Add pepper to taste and breadcrumbs. Leave until cool.

Cut fillo sheets into strips, butter, fold, fill and shape as directed for shaping triangles, using a heaped teaspoon of filling for each triangle.

Place join side down on a lightly greased baking sheet. Repeat with remaining ingredients. Brush tops lightly with butter and bake in a moderately hot oven for 10-12 minutes. Serve hot as an appetiser or snack.

SAUSAGE ROLLS

Makes 18 or 24, depending on size
Oven temperature
190-200°C (375-400°F)

1 medium-sized onion, grated
2 tablespoons finely chopped parsley
1 cup soft breadcrumbs
1 tablespoon tomato sauce
500 g sausage mince
9 sheets fillo pastry
melted butter or substitute

Place grated onion, parsley, crumbs and tomato sauce in a bowl and mix well. Add sausage mince and mix thoroughly. Alternatively place roughly chopped onion, parsley leaves, crumbs and sauce in food processor bowl with steel blade. Process until onion and parsley are finely chopped, add sausage mince and process until combined.

Butter and stack 3 sheets fillo pastry. Butter top of stack. Place a third of the sausage mince in a 4 cm (1½ inch) wide strip towards end of longer edge of pastry. Mound mince and smooth it so that it is about 3 cm (1¼ inches) high. Roll up evenly and firmly. Trim ends and cut roll into 6 or 8 even lengths, depending on size required. Place rolls on lightly greased baking sheets. Repeat with remaining ingredients. Bake in a moderately hot oven for 25 minutes. Serve hot.

FRIED CAMEMBERT TRIANGLES

Makes 18

1 camembert cheese
3 sheets fillo pastry for
Triangles (page 13)
peanut or maize oil for deep frying

Cut cheese into 6 even-sized wedges. Slice each wedge horizontally through the soft centre into 3 pieces to give triangles of cheese about 5 mm (¼ inch) thick. Cut fillo pastry into strips no less than 6 cm (2½ inches) wide. Place a piece of camembert on bottom edge, fold up and seal as directed for Triangles for Frying. Take care that corners of triangles enclose cheese completely. Heat oil until very hot, not fuming, and deep fry 6 triangles at a time, turning them to brown evenly. Remove with a slotted spoon, drain on absorbent paper and serve immediately as a savoury.

To serve as a dessert: Follow above directions, coating cheese pieces with toasted desiccated coconut before enclosing in fillo. Fry and serve hot, 3-4 per serve, with cranberry sauce or jelly on the side.

Note: These pastries freeze very well — follow instructions for Freezer Storage (page 11).

NUT TRIANGLES

Makes 40
Oven temperature
170-180°C (325-350°F)

1 cup ground blanched almonds
½ cup finely chopped cashew nuts
½ cup finely chopped pecans or walnuts
2 egg yolks
½ cup sugar
1 teaspoon rose water or ½ teaspoon
vanilla essence
18 sheets fillo pastry for
Triangles (page 13)
melted butter
icing sugar

Nuts may be prepared in food processor using steel blade. Prepare almonds first and grind finely, but take care not to over-grind as this brings out the oil. Do cashews and pecans or walnuts separately until finely chopped.

Beat egg yolks with sugar until light and creamy. Stir in nuts and rose water or vanilla to make a stiff coarse paste.

Cut each fillo sheet into 18 cm (7 inch) strips, stack and cover. Trim any off-cuts of fillo to 6 cm (2½ inches) wide and add to stack. Brush wide strip of fillo with butter and fold into 3 to give a strip 6 cm (2½ inches) wide. Brush top with butter, fill and fold as directed for Triangles for Baking using a heaped teaspoon of filling for each triangle. To use the off-cuts, butter three strips together, fill and fold up.

Place triangles on greased baking sheets and brush tops lightly with butter. Bake in a moderate oven, one shelf above centre, for 20 minutes or until golden brown. Filling will firm up when pastries cool. Leave on baking sheets and when partly cooled, dust with icing sugar.

CINNAMON STICKS

Makes about 18
Oven temperature
170-180°C (325-350°F)

An ideal way to use left over fillo pastry. Pastry strips left from shaping other pastries may also be used in this way. The sugar caramelizes during cooking, giving a delicious flavour.

½ cup caster sugar
2 tablespoons ground cinnamon
6 sheets fillo pastry
melted butter

Mix caster sugar with cinnamon. Butter a sheet of fillo pastry and fold in half across its length to give a rectangle. Turn folded side toward you. Brush top with butter and sprinkle evenly with 1 tablespoon cinnamon sugar leaving 2 cm (¾ inch) of top edge free of sugar. Roll up from folded side into a firm roll. Cut into 3 equal pieces and reshape ends where cut to keep roll shape. Repeat process with remaining sheets of pastry.

Place completed rolls close together, join side down, on a greased baking sheet. Brush tops with butter and sprinkle with cinnamon sugar. Bake in a moderate oven for 10-12 minutes until crisp and golden brown — take care not to burn them. Cool on a baking sheet and store in a sealed container. Serve as a dessert biscuit with creamy and fruit desserts.
Coconut Sticks Replace cinnamon with ¼ cup desiccated coconut and use a generous tablespoon of the mixture on each sheet of fillo pastry. Sprinkle coconut-sugar mixture on top of buttered rolls before baking. Serve as above or with coffee.

ALMOND FLUTES

Makes 30-35 rolls
Oven temperature
180-190°C (350-375°F)

SYRUP:
½ cup water
¾ cup sugar
2 teaspoons lemon juice
2 teaspoons orange flower water
ALMOND FILLING:
1½ cups coarsely ground
blanched almonds
1 egg white
¼ cup caster sugar
1 teaspoon orange flower water
TO FINISH:
6-7 sheets fillo pastry
melted butter

Make syrup first. Dissolve sugar in water over heat in a small heavy pan, add lemon juice and bring to the boil. Boil, without stirring, for 12 minutes. Add orange flower water, boil 30 seconds and remove from heat. Leave aside to cool.

Coarsely grind the blanched almonds in food processor with steel blade, otherwise finely chop about 1 cup blanched almonds and mix with ground almonds to make 1½ cups. Beat egg white until stiff, beat in sugar, then fold in almonds and orange flower water to form a soft, coarse paste. Keep aside.

Brush a sheet of fillo lightly and evenly with butter. At longer edge, fold up 3 cm (1¼ inches) of the fillo. Take a level tablespoon of filling and put dabs of the filling along the folded fillo, then with a small metal spatula spread filling evenly. Fold up once more and place a 5 mm (¼ inch) dowel along the centre (dowel should be longer than fillo sheet). Roll the end of the folded section around the dowel, then roll up to end of pastry, brushing end with butter if necessary to stick onto roll. Carefully slip roll off the dowel and cut into 5 even pieces. Gently reshape ends of rolls into a round shape after cutting.

Place rolls join side down into greased shallow slab cake pan or baking dish. Make remaining rolls. Brush with melted butter and bake in a moderate oven for 15-20 minutes until golden. When cooked, pour cooled syrup over hot rolls and leave for several hours until cold. Store in a sealed container at room temperature.

There are many interesting adaptations possible with this recipe. Following are three alternative shapings:
Shirred Almond Rolls Thin, pliable fillo pastry must be used for these rolls. Crumple up a sheet in your hand. If you can open it out without tearing, you can make these.

After rolling the nut-filled pastry on the dowel, gently push roll from each end, shirring the pastry on the dowel so that roll is about two-thirds its original length. Even the shirring gently with your fingers. Slip shirred roll off the dowel onto board and cut into even pieces 8-9 cm (3-3½ inches) long. Trim ends. Place rolls in a greased dish, close together, and brush with butter. If there are any gaps between the rolls and the dish, crumple some foil and place next to rolls. If rolls are not close together they lose shape during cooking. Makes 18-21 rolls.
Shirred Almond Rings Make as for Shirred Almond Rolls, cutting shirred roll in half instead of three. Shape into a ring, pressing ends together. Place close together in greased dish, brush with butter, bake and finish as for rolls. Sprinkle with chopped pistachio nuts if desired. Makes 12-14 rings (continued overleaf).

Sultan's Turbans (A Turkish version) Use double quantity of ingredients. Turkish pastries are mostly flavoured with cinnamon rather than orange flower water. Use a piece of cinnamon bark and a thin strip of lemon rind in the syrup, added with the water, and omit orange flower water. Add 1 teaspoon ground cinnamon to the nut filling in place of the orange flower water. Roll as for Shirred Almond Rolls but do not cut shirred roll. Trim ends and gently curl into a flat coil. Place close together in greased dish, brush lightly with butter, bake for 20-25 minutes and pour cooled syrup over hot pastries. Cool, and serve sprinkled with chopped pistachio nuts if desired. Makes 12-14 turbans.

DATE WONTONS

Makes about 24

1 tablespoon butter
¾ cup chopped dates
1 tablespoon brown sugar
¼ cup toasted sesame seeds or chopped walnuts
grated rind of 1 orange
4 sheets fillo pastry for Triangles for Frying (page 13)
oil for deep frying
icing sugar for serving

Melt butter in a heavy pan, add dates and brown sugar and heat, stirring occasionally, until dates soften — about 2 minutes. Turn into a bowl and stir in sesame seeds or walnuts and the grated orange rind. Mix to a stiff paste and leave to cool.

Cut fillo sheets into strips, fill, fold into triangles and seal as directed for Triangles for Frying, using a rounded teaspoon of filling for each pastry. Place finished pastries join side down onto absorbent paper.

Heat oil and deep fry wontons a few at a time until golden brown and crisp, turning to brown evenly. Remove with draining spoon and drain on absorbent paper. Dust with sifted icing sugar and serve hot.

HAZELNUT CHOCOLATE FINGERS

Makes 12
Oven temperature
150-160°C (300-325°F)

½ cup finely ground hazelnuts
⅓ cup caster sugar
6 sheets fillo pastry
melted butter
60 g (2 oz) dark chocolate

Hazelnuts which have not been toasted and skinned should be used as they toast during cooking. Mix ground hazelnuts with caster sugar.

Brush 2 sheets of fillo pastry together with butter. Brush top with butter and sprinkle 1½ tablespoons of the nut mixture on half the pastry. Fold in half across its length and brush top with butter. Again sprinkle with nut mixture, leaving 3 cm (1¼ inches) of pastry at end opposite the fold clear of nut mixture. Turn the folded side towards you and fold up 2 cm (¾ inch) of this side.

Roll up pastry firmly and brush the clear end of the strip again with butter if necessary so that it stays in place. Cut roll carefully into 4 even pieces about 8 cm (3 inches) long. Place on a lightly greased baking sheet, join side down. Make remainder of rolls with the fillo and the nut mixture. Brush tops lightly with butter and bake in a moderately slow oven for 20-25 minutes until crisp and golden — do not overbrown.

Break up chocolate in a heatproof cup measure and place in a pan of gently heating water. Melt, stirring often, so that chocolate does not overheat. Put melted chocolate into the corner of a small plastic bag, snip corner off to make a very small hole and pipe chocolate in a zig-zag along the length of each roll. Leave until set, preferably in a cool place rather than a refrigerator. Store in a sealed container. Serve with after dinner coffee.
Note: On cooling, the outer layer of fillo pastry sometimes flakes. Gently remove the flaked fillo to improve the appearance of the rolls.

BIGGER WRAP-UPS

A fillo-wrapped first or main course has a 'touch of class' about it. With subtle garnish, the ordinary is lifted into the extraordinary; but the advantage to the cook is that most fillo-wrapped foods may be kept refrigerated until it is time to pop them into the oven — a definite advantage when entertaining. Both savoury and sweet foods may be wrapped in the various ways described.

BASIC SHAPING

As these shapes — Large Triangles, Coils, Rolls and Parcels — are mostly baked, instructions for preparation for baking are given; recipes which require frying give specific instructions within the recipe.

Triangles

Cut fillo sheets in 3 even strips along their length to give strips about 10 cm (4 inches) wide and 40-50 cm (16-20 inches) long. Stack and cover with dry and damp cloths. Brush with melted butter, place about 2 tablespoons filling on lower edge and fold up into a triangle, following directions given for small triangles (Little Wrap-ups, page 13).

Coils

Coils can only be made if fillo is soft and pliable. Brush a fillo sheet with butter or oil and fold in half across its width, to give a strip 15 cm (6 inches) wide and as long as the fillo sheet. Brush top with water. With folded edge towards you, place about 2 tablespoonfuls filling in a strip 3 cm (1¼ inches) in from base and sides. Fold base of fillo over the filling and fold in sides. Roll to end of pastry and with join side down, gently curl into a flat coil. Place on a greased baking sheet and brush top with butter or oil.

Rolls

Ideal for soft fillings which can be shaped into a cylinder, and for cylindrically shaped foods such as rolled ham and asparagus.

Roll I Brush fillo sheet lightly with butter and fold in half across the length to give a rectangle 20-25 cm (8-10 inches) wide and 30 cm (12 inches) long. Brush top with butter. With narrow end towards you, place 2-3 tablespoons filling towards the bottom edge, keeping filling 3 cm (1¼ inches) in from base and sides of pastry. Fold bottom of pastry over filling, fold in sides and roll up to end of strip. Place join side down onto a greased baking sheet and brush top with butter.

Roll II Prepare and fold sheet as for Roll I. Lightly butter top and place filling across one corner, in from the sides. Fold corner over filling, turn once, fold in sides and roll to opposite corner. Place join side down on greased baking sheet and brush top with butter.

Parcels

These wraps are used for foods of a definite irregular shape, such as chicken fillets, steaks and fish fillets.

Parcel I Brush a sheet of fillo with butter and top with another sheet. Butter, fold in half across the length and brush top with butter. Place food across one corner of pastry, fold corner over food, fold in sides and fold up to end. If food has a topping, food must be so wrapped that the topping remains at the top in the finished parcel.

With some food items, the width of the rectangle is sometimes insufficient. To increase the width, do not fold in half; instead fold pastry so that one edge is about 5 cm (2 inches) in from the other. (See illustration page 29.)

Parcel II Prepare as for Parcel I, extending width of rectangle if necessary. If fillo sheets are very thin, it may be necessary to use 3 sheets instead of 2 to increase the thickness of the pastry under the food. Brush top with butter. With folded edge to one side, place food in the centre of wrap. Bring bottom and top of pastry together over the food, buttered sides together. Make a double fold and press flat over food. Fold in corners at sides and tuck sides under parcel.

Using less fat For Roll II, Parcel I and Parcel II do not butter the sheets together. Brush top sheet lightly with butter and fold. Brush lightly with butter and proceed with roll or parcel.

Advance Preparation of Pastries

Most of the recipes in this chapter may be prepared ahead and held in the refrigerator for several hours before cooking and serving. While many recipes do give directions in this regard, as a general rule pastries containing a very moist filling are better cooked as soon after wrapping as possible.

With regard to freezing these large wrapped pastries, all but those containing beef, lamb and pork may be frozen, see Freezer Storage of Pastries (page 11). As meats are only browned and not cooked through in the initial stages of preparation, the freezing and subsequent thawing of such wrapped foods causes excessive drip, making the pastry soggy and the meat dry.

Serving Sauces

Recipes direct that sauces be served separately or at the side of the fillo-wrapped food. The reason is that fillo pastry can lose its characteristic crispness quickly if sauce is poured on top.

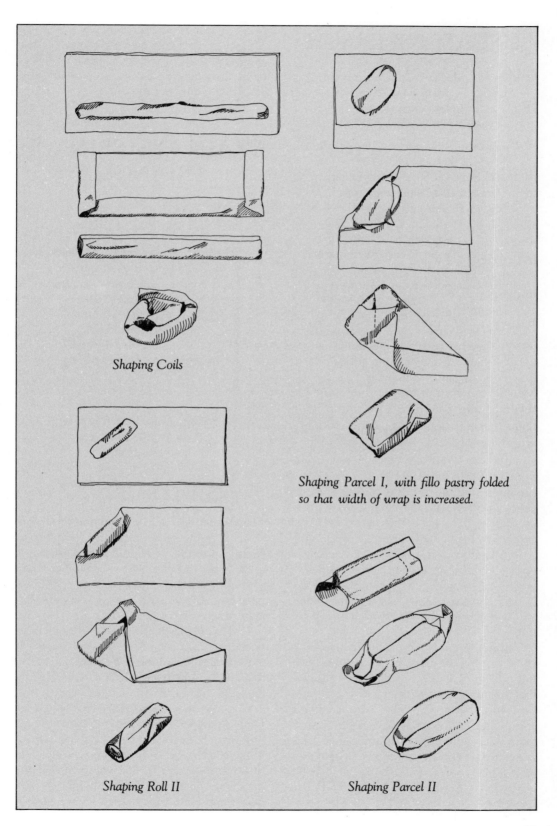

Shaping Coils

Shaping Parcel I, with fillo pastry folded
so that width of wrap is increased.

Shaping Roll II

Shaping Parcel II

CREAMY SPINACH COILS

Makes 18-20
Oven temperature
180-190°C (350-375°F)

1 bunch spinach, about 750 g (1½ lbs)
2 tablespoons butter
1½ cups chopped spring onions,
including some green tops
250 g (8 oz) packaged cream cheese at
room temperature
2 eggs, lightly beaten
¼ cup grated romano or parmesan cheese
¼ cup chopped parsley
¼ teaspoon ground nutmeg
salt
freshly ground pepper
20 sheets fillo pastry for Coils (page 27)
melted butter or substitute
additional tablespoon grated
parmesan cheese
paprika

Trim roots from spinach. Wash leaves and stalks well and chop roughly. Place in a large pan, cover and leave over medium heat for 5 minutes to wilt spinach, tossing spinach occasionally. When wilted turn into colander and press out moisture with the back of a spoon. Turn onto a board and chop coarsely. Melt butter in a pan, add spring onions and cook gently until soft, but still green. Keep aside.

In a large mixing bowl work cream cheese until soft using a wooden spoon. Gradually beat in eggs and grated cheese. Add chopped spinach, spring onions, parsley and nutmeg and mix thoroughly. Add salt and pepper to taste.

Using fillo pastry and melted butter make coils as directed with about 2 tablespoons spinach filling for each coil. Place coils close together in a greased baking dish and brush tops with butter. Sprinkle with additional cheese and a little paprika. Bake in a moderately hot oven for 25-30 minutes until golden and puffed. Serve hot or warm as a light meal, or as a first course. These freeze well. Follow instructions for Freezer Storage of Pastries (page 11).

Note: If fresh spinach is out of season, use two 250 g (8 oz) packets frozen leaf spinach. Thaw and drain well. Silverbeet (Swiss chard) may be used though the flavour is quite different. Use leaves only, not the stalks.

BRAIN AND SPINACH TRIANGLES

Makes about 12
Oven temperature
190-200°C (375-400°F)

250 g (8 oz) packet frozen leaf spinach
or 1 cup fresh cooked spinach
3 sets cooked lamb brains (see Brain
Tricorns, page 16)
1 cup chopped spring onions
2 tablespoons butter
1 tablespoon chopped parsley
¼ teaspoon ground nutmeg
1 egg
¼ cup sour cream
salt
freshly ground black pepper
8 sheets fillo for Large
Triangles (page 27)
melted butter or substitute
toasted sesame seeds, optional
Lemon Sauce for serving (page 31)

Thaw frozen leaf spinach and drain well in a sieve, pressing with the back of a spoon to extract moisture. If freshly cooked spinach is used, drain likewise before measuring. Chop spinach fairly finely and place in a bowl. Cook lamb brains as directed, cool and cut into dice. Add to spinach.

In a frying pan gently cook spring onions in butter until soft but still green. Add to spinach with parsley and nutmeg. Beat egg and stir in sour cream. Add to spinach mixture, mix lightly and season to taste with salt and pepper.

Cut fillo sheets into strips as directed for Large Triangles. Butter 2 strips together, brush top with butter and place 2 tablespoons of filling on one end. Fold up into a triangle (see illustration, page 29). Place finished triangles on a greased baking sheet and brush tops with butter. Sprinkle with toasted sesame seeds if desired. Bake in a preheated moderately hot oven for 20 minutes or until puffed and golden. Serve hot, 2 per serve, as a light meal, or 1 per serve as a first course. Lemon Sauce should be served separately, or at the side of the pastries.

LEMON SAUCE

Makes about 1½ cups

1 tablespoon butter
1 tablespoon flour
¾ cup chicken stock
grated rind of 1 lemon
2 eggs
1-2 tablespoons lemon juice
salt
freshly ground white pepper

Melt butter in a small saucepan, stir in flour and cook gently for 2 minutes. Pour in chicken stock and, stirring constantly, bring to the boil. Add grated lemon rind. Let sauce boil gently. Beat eggs in a bowl until foamy, beat in 1 tablespoon lemon juice, then gradually pour in hot stock beating constantly. Add more lemon juice if necessary and season to taste. Return to pan and stir over gentle heat for 2 minutes until thick. Remove from heat and keep stirring for a minute or so to prevent heat of pan curdling the sauce. Cover and keep warm by setting pan in pan of fairly hot water (do not overheat). Serve as directed in recipes.

SMOKED SALMON BLINTZES

Makes 6

A Blintze is a thin pancake, filled, shaped into a flat parcel and fried in butter. Fillo makes a delightful substitute for the pancake.

6 thin slices smoked salmon
½ cup ricotta cheese or sieved cottage cheese
¼ cup sour cream
¼ cup chopped chives or spring onions
freshly ground pepper
6 sheets fillo pastry
melted butter
oil and clarified butter for frying
sour cream and caviar for serving
spring onion curls

Salmon slices should be about 8 × 12 cm (3 × 5 inches) in size. Mix cheese (preferably ricotta) with cream and chives or spring onions. Add pepper to taste.

Brush a fillo sheet lightly with butter and fold in half across its length and brush again with butter. Place a slice of salmon on one narrow end and spread a tablespoon of cheese mixture on one half. Fold salmon over onto filling, then fold in base and sides of pastry over salmon. Brush folds lightly with butter and fold up into a flat parcel, rectangular in shape.

Put oil and clarified butter (same butter as used for brushing pastry) in a frying pan to a depth of 5 mm (¼ inch), heat well and add parcels. Shallow fry for 3-4 minutes, turning carefully with an egg lifter to brown evenly. Take care not to pierce wrapping. Remove to absorbent paper to drain. Serve hot as a first course with sour cream and caviar (lumpfish caviar is fine for this), or serve plain with spring onion curls as garnish.

Note: Smoked Salmon Blintzes can be served as a light meal — allow 2 or 3 per person. Also if you like to avoid fried foods, brush the blintzes with butter and bake in a pre-heated oven 210-220°C (425-450°F) for 7-8 minutes. While blintzes are far from low calorie fare, you will eliminate quite a few of them by baking rather than frying.

MOUSSELINE OF SEAFOOD EVANS

Serves 6
Oven temperature
200-210°C (400-425°F)

Len Evans, wine buff, raconteur and food and wine writer, was the source for this delicately flavoured mousseline. He has a penchant for easy starters using fillo pastry — shows what good taste he has! The skeleton of this recipe appeared in his magazine column — in pedantic fashion I have given you quantities of ingredients.

250 g (8 oz) fresh shelled scallops
with coral
250 g (8 oz) shelled green prawns,
deveined
2 egg whites (from medium-sized eggs)
2-3 tablespoons cream
1 teaspoon salt
freshly ground white pepper
12 sheets fillo pastry for Roll II (page 27)
Nantua Sauce (page 32)

Clean dark veins from scallops. Rinse prawns after deveining and dry scallops and prawns with absorbent paper. Place in food processor bowl with steel blade fitted, add egg white and process until smooth. Blend in cream, only adding enough for paste to hold its form — it will be soft, but not liquid. Add salt and pepper to taste.

Butter together 2 sheets fillo pastry. Butter top and fold in half. Brush again with butter and place about 3 tablespoons filling across one corner, and in from sides. Smooth with a spatula into a rounded strip so that filling is of even thickness. Fold corner of pastry loosely over filling, fold in sides and brush folded sides with butter. Roll loosely to end of pastry. (The mousseline puffs during cooking and a little care in shaping the mixture and rolling it up helps to keep the completed pastries in a good shape after cooking.) Prepare remaining rolls.

Place finished rolls on a greased baking sheet and brush tops and sides lightly with butter. Bake in a preheated hot oven for 15 minutes until puffed and golden. Serve hot with Nantua Sauce.

BECHAMEL SAUCE

1½ cups milk
1 small onion, chopped
1 small carrot, chopped
1 small bay leaf
1 sprig parsley
½ teaspoon whole peppercorns
2 tablespoons butter
2 tablespoons flour
salt to taste

Place milk in a saucepan with onion, carrot, bay leaf, parsley and peppercorns. Slowly bring to the boil and let milk simmer gently for 5 minutes — keep heat very low and stir occasionally to prevent it boiling over. Strain milk into a jug.

In a clean, heavy pan melt butter and stir in flour. Cook gently for 2 minutes or so without colouring roux, then pour hot milk in gradually, stirring constantly. When thickened and boiling, season to taste with salt and let sauce simmer gently for 5 minutes. Use as directed in recipes.

NANTUA SAUCE

1 quantity Bechamel Sauce (page 32)
2 tablespoons butter
¼ cup chopped cooked prawns
½ teaspoon anchovy essence
1 teaspoon lemon juice

Make Bechamel Sauce as directed and leave to simmer gently. Put butter and prawns in food processor bowl with steel blade. Add anchovy essence and lemon juice. Process until smooth, scraping down bowl when necessary. Gradually stir this prawn butter into the simmering sauce. Adjust seasoning and add a little more lemon juice if desired. Strain into sauce boat and serve with Mousseline of Seafood Evans or with other seafood dishes.

SMOKED TROUT WITH HORSERADISH CREAM SAUCE

Serves 6
Oven temperature
210-220°C (425-450°F)

3 smoked trout, each about 200 g (7 oz)
small sprigs of fresh dill
6 sheets fillo pastry for Parcel I (page 28)
melted butter
small drained capers and dill sprigs
to garnish
HORSERADISH CREAM SAUCE:
1 cup thick sour cream
2 teaspoons chopped fresh dill
2 tablespoons prepared horseradish
salt
freshly ground white pepper
2 egg yolks, optional

Carefully remove skin from trout and lift fillets from the bones on each side of the fish. There will be 6 fillets. Remove flat bones from fillets, and if possible pull out bones running through centre of fillets. Top each fillet with 2 small sprigs of fresh dill.

Brush a sheet of fillo with melted butter and fold in half. Brush top with butter and place fillet across one corner of sheet and in from sides. Fold corner of pastry over fish, fold in sides and wrap to end of pastry. Place join side down on a greased baking sheet. Wrap remaining fish. Brush tops lightly with butter and bake in a pre-heated hot oven for 8 minutes to crisp the pastry. Spoon sauce onto warmed small plates and place trout packets in the centre. Garnish with capers and dill sprigs.

Horseradish Cream Sauce Put sour cream in a small saucepan and stir in dill, horseradish and salt and pepper to taste. Heat, stirring often, until heated through. Sauce will be thin. If desired, mix egg yolks into sauce before beginning to heat and stir constantly over heat until egg thickens the sauce. Do not boil.

FRIED FILLOED FISH

Fish fried in a thin, crisp coating of batter! The most popular way to eat fish — whether counting calories or not. More cooks would prepare fish in this way at home if it were not for the fumes which batter-frying creates. When I discovered that fillo makes a crisp, light coating on fish fillets I was delighted, because fillo fries without any fuss — in fact it cooks so quietly that you wonder if it is cooking at all! Thin fish fillets cook best — in fact I recommend only thin fillets. If fillets are very thick, slit through the middle to reduce bulk.

thin fish fillets such as snapper, bream,
whiting, John Dory
½-1 sheet fillo pastry for each fillet
flour, seasoned with salt and pepper
oil for shallow frying

Remove skin from fish fillets if present. Dry fillets with absorbent paper. Open out fillo sheets and remove number required, allowing half a sheet for small fillets, a whole sheet for large. Return unused fillo to pack. Cut fillo sheets in half if necessary, stack and cover.

Coat fish fillet with seasoned flour, shake off excess and place towards one corner of fillo sheet, in from the sides. Fold end of fillo over fish, fold in sides and brush side folds and opposite corner lightly with water. Wrap into a neat parcel. Do not try to keep to the shape of fillet — the parcel will be rectangular in shape and as wide as the widest part of the fillet. Place fold side down onto absorbent paper until all fillets are wrapped.

Heat oil for shallow frying in a large frying pan, adding oil to a depth of 5 mm (¼ inch). When hot, add fish fillets (fold side down first) and fry for 3-5 minutes on each side, depending on thickness of fillets. Fish will not sizzle, so do not be tempted to increase heat — just check that fillo is browning. Turn carefully with 2 wide metal spatulas so as not to pierce fillo. When golden brown, remove and drain on absorbent paper. Serve with lemon wedges or tartare sauce.

TARRAGON FISH WITH AVOCADO

Serves 6
Oven temperature
190-200°C (375-400°F)

750 g (1½ lb) thick fish fillets such
as ling, flathead, hake, cod
1 large ripe avocado
lemon juice
1 tablespoon chopped fresh tarragon
salt
freshly ground black pepper
12 sheets fillo pastry for
Parcel I (page 28)
melted butter
tarragon sprigs to garnish
Lemon Sauce (page 31) for serving

Remove skin from fillets if present, and if time permits remove any bones with tweezers. Rinse if necessary and dry with absorbent paper. Cut fillets into 12 thick strips about 4-5 cm (1½-2 inches) wide and 8-10 cm (4-5 inches) long. Halve avocado, remove seed and peel. Cut each half into 6 wedges, along the length of the avocado. Place fish and avocado on separate plates, and sprinkle both with lemon juice. Sprinkle tarragon, salt and pepper onto fish.

Butter together 2 sheets fillo pastry, fold in half and butter top. Place 2 strips of fish across one corner and in from sides and insert 2 wedges of avocado between the fish strips. Fold corner of fillo over fish, fold in sides and brush side folds with butter. Complete wrap and place join side down onto a greased baking sheet. Make remaining parcels in the same way. Parcels may be covered and refrigerated for several hours at this stage.

To bake, place in a preheated moderately hot oven and cook for 18-20 minutes until golden brown. Fish is cooked when juices begin to sizzle on baking sheet. Serve hot, garnished with tarragon sprigs with Lemon Sauce served separately. Make Lemon Sauce with fish stock instead of the chicken stock — fish stock cubes are available.
Note: Only use French tarragon for this recipe. The other tarragon readily available is Russian tarragon and this is only suitable for garnishing.

If fresh French tarragon is unavailable or out of season, then use 1 teaspoon dried tarragon, rubbed to a coarse powder.

PRAWNS PIRAEUS

Serves 6
Oven temperature
190-200°C (374-400°F)

750 g (1½ lbs) cooked prawns
1 cup chopped spring onions
2 tablespoons olive oil
2 cloves garlic, crushed
425 g (15 oz) can peeled tomatoes,
chopped
¼ cup dry white wine
½ teaspoon dried marjoram
½ teaspoon sugar
salt and pepper
2 tablespoons chopped parsley
2 tablespoons chopped chives
125 g (4 oz) feta cheese
12 sheets fillo pastry for Parcel II
(page 28)
melted butter or olive oil
6 whole unpeeled prawns and
chive tops to garnish

Shell prawns, devein and rinse. Dry with absorbent paper, place in a bowl, cover and refrigerate until required.

Cook spring onion in olive oil until soft but still green, add garlic, cook a few seconds, then stir in tomatoes, wine, marjoram, sugar and salt and pepper to taste. Use very little salt as the feta is salty. Boil gently, uncovered, until reduced to a thick sauce — thick enough so that it holds its shape when dropped from a spoon. Remove from heat, stir in parsley and chives and leave until cool.

Cut feta cheese into 1 cm (½ inch) dice and add to tomato sauce with prawns. Adjust seasoning. (continued page 37)

Apricot Lamb in Fillo (page 42), in preparation.

Butter or oil 2 sheets fillo pastry together, brush top lightly with butter and fold almost in half to give an enlarged rectangle of pastry. Spoon a sixth of the prawn mixture into the centre and shape it into a square about 1 cm (½ inch) thick. Bring the two long sides together and double fold pastry over top, fold in corners at sides and tuck sides underneath parcel (see directions for Parcel II). Make other parcels with filling and fillo pastry.

Place parcels on a greased baking sheet and brush tops and sides lightly with butter or oil and bake in a pre-heated moderately hot oven for 20 minutes or until puffed and golden. Serve hot, garnishing each plate with a whole, unshelled prawn with a few slender chive tops in a little bundle tucked into curve of prawn.

CHINESE CHICKEN AND HAM ROLLS

Serves 6 as a main meal, 12 as an appetiser or snack

6 large chicken fillets (3 whole breasts, boned and halved)
1 clove garlic, crushed (optional)
1 teaspoon salt
¼ teaspoon Chinese five spice powder
½ teaspoon ground pepper
6 thin slices leg ham
1 egg
1 tablespoon milk
about ¼ cup cornflour
6 sheets fillo pastry for Roll II (page 27)
oil for deep frying
FOR SERVING:
lettuce leaves or shredded lettuce
Chili Sauce (page 21)
or Plum Sauce (page 22)

Remove skin from chicken fillets if present. Place each fillet between 2 sheets of plastic film and flatten carefully with a meat mallet or the side of a cleaver.

Chicken and Avocado Puffs (page 38), in preparation.

Place chicken flat on a board with inside surface uppermost. If using garlic, rub a little over the surface of each breast. Mix salt with five spice powder and pepper. Sprinkle evenly over the chicken. Remove excess fat from ham edge and roll up firmly. Place ham roll on one long side of chicken and roll chicken up firmly, tucking in ragged sides of breast. Leave rolls join side down.

Fold each fillo sheet in half to give a rectangle, stack and cover with a dry cloth.

Beat egg with milk in a shallow dish. Coat chicken rolls with egg, then with cornflour and again place on a board with join side down.

Place a chicken roll across one corner, as directed for Roll II, with the folded side on one side of the corner. Turn corner of pastry over chicken, fold in sides, and roll one turn. Brush the long flap of pastry lightly with cold water also brushing lightly between the two leaves at the far corner of the folded sheet. Complete the roll and place roll join side down onto absorbent paper. Repeat with remaining chicken rolls and fillo.

Heat oil until very hot but not fuming and fry rolls one or two at a time, turning to brown evenly. Cook for 5-6 minutes so that chicken is completely cooked. Oil has to be hot enough to fry rolls, but not too hot as fillo will over-brown before chicken is cooked. Fillo wrapped pastries do not cause the oil to bubble as much as spring roll wrappers. A good indication that chicken is cooked is when oil begins to spatter from the escaping chicken juices. Leave in oil for another 30 seconds when this happens.

Drain rolls on absorbent paper and serve whole, or cut in diagonal slices. Serve with crisp lettuce leaves or shredded lettuce and Chili or Plum Sauce.

Chinese Chicken and Crab Rolls Make as above, replacing ham with 6 thawed seafood or crab sticks (these are pressed seafoods or crab shaped into sticks 12 cm or 5 inches long and are available frozen). Prepare, roll in fillo, fry and serve as for Chicken and Ham Rolls.

CHICKEN AND AVOCADO PUFFS

Serves 6
Oven temperature
180-190°C (350-375°F)

2 tablespoons flour
salt
freshly ground pepper
2 tablespoons ground almonds
6 large chicken fillets (boneless chicken
from 3 whole breasts)
1 tablespoon butter
1 tablespoon oil
1 medium-sized ripe avocado
1 tablespoon lemon juice
12 sheets fillo pastry for
Parcel II (page 28)
melted butter or substitute
SHERRY CREAM SAUCE:
1½ tablespoons flour-almond mixture
from chicken coating
½ cup strong chicken stock
2 tablespoons dry sherry
¼ cup cream
about 1 tablespoon lemon juice

Mix flour with 1 teaspoon salt, pepper to taste, and ground almonds. Remove skin from chicken fillets if necessary. Coat chicken with flour mixture. Heat butter and oil in a frying pan until foaming and brown chicken on each side — do not cook through. Remove chicken to a plate and leave until cool. Drain any juices back into pan and reserve pan drippings for sauce. Mash avocado flesh and mix with lemon juice and salt and pepper to taste.

Prepare fillo sheets as directed, buttering top of rectangle with butter. Place a chicken fillet in centre of wrap and spread top with a sixth of the avocado mixture. Complete wrap as directed for Parcel II. Place join side down on a lightly greased baking sheet. Repeat with remaining ingredients. Brush packets lightly on top and sides with melted butter. Bake in a pre-heated moderately hot oven for 20 minutes. Serve with Sherry Cream Sauce.

Sherry Cream Sauce Heat pan in which chicken was cooked to evaporate any liquid. Add a little more butter if needed and sprinkle in flour-almond mixture, making it up to 1½ tablespoons with flour if necessary. Cook 1 minute on moderate heat and add chicken stock and sherry, stirring constantly. When thickened and bubbling stir in cream and lemon juice. Heat a little longer and pour into a sauce boat.

Note: If chicken fillets are small, use 2 for each parcel. Avocado may be sliced in thin wedges and sprinkled with lemon juice, salt and pepper. Place 2 slices avocado between 2 overlapping chicken fillets for each parcel.

MANGO CHICKEN ROLLS

Serves 6
Oven temperature
180-190°C (350-375°F)

6 large chicken fillets (boneless
chicken from 3 whole breasts)
1 fresh mango or 6 canned mango slices
2 tablespoons flour
1 teaspoon brown sugar
1 teaspoon mustard powder
grated rind of 1 orange
½ teaspoon salt
1 tablespoon butter
1 tablespoon oil
12 sheets fillo pastry for
Parcel I (page 28)
melted butter or substitute
ORANGE PORT SAUCE:
flour mixture left from coating chicken
½ cup orange juice
2-3 tablespoons port
1 chicken stock cube
2 tablespoons cream

Remove skin from chicken fillets if present. Flatten each fillet carefully between 2 sheets of plastic film using a meat mallet or the side of a cleaver. Cut peeled mango into 6 even-sized wedges, or drain and dry canned mango slices. Roll a mango slice inside each fillet. Secure with wooden cocktail picks — the ends need not be secured.

Mix flour thoroughly with sugar, mustard, orange rind and salt. Coat chicken rolls lightly with this mixture. Heat oil and butter in a frying pan and lightly brown chicken on all sides. Do not cook through. Remove to a plate and leave until cool. Keep pan drippings and any flour mixture for sauce. Remove cocktail picks from chicken when cold.

Take 2 fillo sheets and lightly butter them together. Butter top, fold in half and butter again. Place a chicken roll across one corner, fold over base and sides of pastry and brush folds with butter. Roll to end. Place on greased baking sheet join side down and brush top lightly with butter. Repeat with remaining ingredients. Bake in a moderately hot oven for 20 minutes. Serve hot with Orange Port Sauce.

Orange Port Sauce Make up any remaining flour mixture to 3 teaspoons with plain flour if necessary. Heat pan in which fillets were browned and stir in flour. Cook 1 minute then stir in orange juice and port to taste. When thickened add crumbled stock cube and stir until dissolved. Add salt and pepper to taste, simmer gently 1 minute, stir in cream, then strain into sauceboat. Pour a little at the side of each roll.

Note: After rolls have been placed on baking sheet and brushed with butter, they may be covered and refrigerated for several hours. Bring to room temperature about 1 hour before baking.

VEAL CORDON BLEU

Serves 6
Oven temperature
200-210°C (400-425°F)

All manner of fillings can be enclosed in thin veal steaks and finished in a fillo crust — again ideal for special occasion meals when you like to do as much as possible ahead of time. Veal Cordon Bleu is a very basic veal dish which is normally crumbed and fried. Fat content is far lower when baked and the filled steaks are much easier to handle. Once you have mastered the technique, you can try other fillings in the veal. Some suggestions are given at the end of the recipe.

6 large thin veal steaks, as oval
in shape as possible
6 thin slices leg ham
6 thin slices Gruyère or Swiss cheese
1 tablespoon oil
1 tablespoon butter
freshly ground pepper
salt
12 sheets fillo pastry for
Parcel I (page 28)
melted butter

Flatten veal steaks if necessary between 2 sheets of plastic film. Nick skin around edges of veal to prevent them from curling. Lay steaks flat on board. The ham and cheese slices should be a little smaller than half the size of the steaks. Place a ham slice on one half of each steak and top with a slice of cheese. Fold steak over and beat edges of steak together lightly with a meat mallet. Secure opening with poultry skewers and season with pepper.

Heat oil and butter in a large frying pan until foaming. Add steaks and sear quickly over high heat for a minute each side or less. Remove to a plate and leave until cool. Remove skewers and season lightly with salt if desired, though ham and cheese provide sufficient salt.

Brush a sheet of fillo lightly with butter, top with another sheet and brush top with butter. Fold almost in half to give a large rectangle. Brush again with butter. Place veal towards one corner, fold corner of pastry over veal, fold in sides and brush folds with butter. Fold up into a parcel. Repeat with remaining steaks and fillo. Place on a lightly greased baking sheet and bake in a hot oven for 12 minutes.

Suggestions for alternative fillings:

Mozzarella, Tomato and Basil Veal Fill steaks with a slice of mozzarella cheese, a slice of tomato sprinkled with salt, pepper and a little dried basil (fresh basil does not work well in this), and some chopped anchovy fillets.

Camembert Veal Cut a camembert cheese into 6 wedges. Slit each wedge in half and flatten pieces a little. Place 2 pieces of cheese on each piece of veal and sprinkle with some chopped toasted almonds.

Apricot Nut Veal Prepare Apricot and Nut stuffing (see Apricot Lamb in Fillo, page 42). Spread 2 tablespoons of filling on each steak.

BEEF STILTON

Serves 6
Oven temperature
200-210°C (400-425°F)

6 fillet steaks cut 4 cm (1½ inches) thick
¼ cup port
freshly ground black pepper
2 tablespoons butter
3 spring onions, chopped
1 cup chopped mushrooms
½ cup soft breadcrumbs
125 g (4 oz) stilton or other blue
vein cheese
12 sheets fillo pastry for
Parcel II (page 28)
melted butter or substitute

Trim fat and visible silver skin from sides of steaks if necessary. Place in a shallow dish, pour port over steaks, cover and marinate for several hours or overnight in refrigerator. Remove and drain well, reserving port. Season steaks with pepper.

Heat butter until foaming and sear steaks on each side until browned. Using tongs or 2 spoons to hold them, sear sides of steaks also. Do not cook through. Remove steaks, drain and place on a rack set on a plate to cool completely.

To butter left in pan add spring onions and mushrooms and sauté on low heat until soft. Increase heat, add reserved port marinade and boil until very little liquid remains. Stir in breadcrumbs. Crumble cheese into a bowl, add contents of pan and mix until combined.

When steaks are completely cold, cut a diagonal slash across the top of each steak, and three parts of the way through. Juices will not run when steak is cold. Fill slashes with the cheese mixture and wrap each steak in buttered fillo as directed for Parcel II. Place on a lightly greased baking sheet. Repeat with remaining ingredients. Lightly brush tops and sides of fillo with butter and bake in a preheated hot oven for 12 minutes for medium rare steak, 15 minutes for medium steak. Serve hot.
Note: Wrapped steaks, with tops and sides buttered, may be covered and held in the refrigerator for up to 8 hours before cooking. Bring to room temperature 1 hour before baking.

PRUNED PORK PACKETS

Serves 6
Oven temperature
180-190°C (350-375°F)

6 thick butterfly pork chops
12 soft pitted dessert prunes
grated rind of 1 lemon
1 tablespoon lemon juice
1 tablespoon butter or oil
salt and pepper
12 sheets fillo pastry
melted butter
SAUCE:
½ cup apple cider
¼ cup chicken stock
3 teaspoons cornflour
¼ cup sour cream

Butterfly chops are cut from the loin. If unavailable, purchase loin chops 3 cm (1¼ inch) thick without the fillet on them, remove the bone and trim the tail.

Place prunes in a small bowl with the lemon rind and juice and leave to soak for 10 minutes or so. Trim most of fat from pork and cut a pocket in each chop if loin chops are being used. Place 2 prunes in pocket. (If using butterfly pork chops, place 2 prunes on one side and fold chop over to enclose.) Secure openings with poultry skewers and season with pepper.

Heat oil in a frying pan until very hot, add chops and sear quickly on each side — just long enough to lightly brown them. Remove to a plate and leave until cool. Remove skewers when cold. Keep aside pan in which chops have been browned.

Brush 2 sheets fillo pastry together with butter and butter top. Place pork across one corner, in from side, turn corner over pork and fold in sides. Wrap to end of sheet and place on a lightly greased baking sheet. Wrap remaining chops. Bake in a pre-heated moderately hot oven for 15-18 minutes, depending on thickness of chops. Serve hot with the sauce.
Sauce Remove fat from pan in which chops were browned, leaving sediment. Heat pan and pour in cider and stock. Stir well to lift browned sediment. Mix cornflour with a little

cold water and stir into liquid, stirring constantly. When thickened and bubbling add salt and pepper to taste and stir in cream. Strain into sauce boat.

BAGGED CARPETBAG STEAKS

Serves 6
Oven temperature
200-210°C (400-425°F)

6 fillet steaks cut 4 cm (1½ inches) thick
12-18 shelled oysters, depending on size
1 teaspoon lemon juice
freshly ground black pepper
2 tablespoons butter
salt
12 sheets fillo pastry for
Parcel I (page 28)
melted butter or substitute

Trim visible silver skin and fat from steaks if necessary. Drain oysters and sprinkle with lemon juice and pepper. Cut a pocket through the side of each steak. Insert 2 or 3 oysters into each steak and secure opening with poultry skewers.

Season steaks with pepper. Heat butter in a frying pan until foaming and sear steaks quickly on each side over high heat, turning with blunt-ended tongs or 2 spoons. Brown sides of steaks also, but do not cook through. Remove to a plate and leave until cool. When cold remove skewers, dry steaks with absorbent paper and season lightly with salt.

Wrap steaks in buttered fillo sheets as directed for Parcel I. Place join side down on a lightly greased baking sheet and brush tops with butter. Bake in a preheated hot oven for 12 minutes for medium rare steak, 2 minutes longer for medium. Serve immediately.
Note: Wrapped steaks, with tops buttered, may be held in refrigerator for up to 8 hours before required. Bring to room temperature for 1 hour before baking.

SPRING ROLLS

Makes 8

250 g (8 oz) boneless pork
1 tablespoon peanut oil
1 teaspoon grated fresh ginger
1 clove garlic, finely chopped
6 spring onions, chopped
1 cup finely chopped mushrooms
½ cup finely chopped bamboo shoots
8 water chestnuts, finely chopped
3 teaspoons soy sauce
2 teaspoons oyster sauce
2 teaspoons cornflour
185 g (6 oz) can shrimp or 185 g (6 oz)
cooked shelled prawns
freshly ground black pepper
8 sheets fillo pastry
peanut oil for deep frying

Use pork fillet or lean meat cut from chops. Finely chop or mince the pork. Heat oil in a pan, add ginger and garlic, cook a few seconds then add pork. Stir over heat until colour changes. Add spring onions and mushrooms and cook until soft. Mix in bamboo shoots and chestnuts. Blend soy and oyster sauces with cornflour and stir into pan contents. Cook until thickened, remove from heat and leave until cool.

Take a sheet of fillo and fold in half to make almost a square shape. Place about 2 tablespoons filling along one corner, in from sides, fold corner over filling and fold in sides. Brush folded sides very lightly with water and lightly brush end of roll, between the folds and on top, with water. (The idea is to soften the fillo slightly so that it will stick in place — too much water and the fillo might break apart.) Complete roll and place join side down onto a cloth. Cover completed rolls with a dry cloth until all are prepared.

Heat oil for deep frying and fry 2-3 rolls at a time, turning to brown evenly. Remove with a draining spoon and drain on absorbent paper. Serve hot.
Note: Spring rolls may be fried ahead of time and reheated in a moderately hot oven for 8-10 minutes.

HAM AND ASPARAGUS ROLLS WITH EGG SAUCE

Serves 6
Oven temperature
200-210°C (400-425°F)

425 g (15 oz) can green asparagus spears
12 thin slices pressed leg ham
6 sheets fillo pastry for Roll II (page 27)
melted butter or substitute
freshly ground pepper
EGG SAUCE:
2 tablespoons butter
2 tablespoons flour
1 teaspoon mustard powder, optional
1 cup milk
salt
freshly ground white pepper
3 hard boiled eggs, quartered or chopped

Drain asparagus and spread spears onto absorbent paper to drain thoroughly. Ham slices can be round or square; if round it may be necessary to remove skin and excess fat.

Brush a sheet of fillo with butter, fold in half and butter top. Overlap 2 slices ham on one corner and place 4-5 asparagus spears along centre. Season with pepper and roll ham around asparagus. Turn corner of pastry over ham roll, fold in sides and roll to end. Place join side down onto greased baking sheet. Make remaining rolls. Bake in a pre-heated hot oven for 10 minutes. Serve hot with Egg Sauce as a light meal.

Egg Sauce Melt butter in a small pan, stir in flour and mustard if used and cook for 2 minutes on low heat. Add milk all at once, stirring constantly. Increase heat and stir until sauce thickens and bubbles. Boil gently for 1 minute, season with salt and pepper and gently fold in hard boiled eggs. Warm through gently and serve directly onto rolls or pour into a sauce boat and serve separately.

APRICOT LAMB IN FILLO

Serves 6
Oven temperature
180-190°C (350-375°F)

6 double lamb cutlets (Frenched rib chops, each with 2 ribs)
freshly ground black pepper
1 tablespoon oil
salt
½ cup chopped dried apricots
1 tablespoon dry sherry
1 tablespoon butter
1 small onion, finely chopped
½ teaspoon curry powder
¼ cup chopped blanched almonds
or cashew nuts
½ cup soft breadcrumbs
1 teaspoon brown sugar
grated rind of ½ lemon
12 sheets fillo pastry
melted butter or substitute

Trim excess fat from lamb and carefully remove one of the rib bones leaving each chop with one bone. Trim any meat and fat from ends of remaining bones. Season meat with pepper. Heat oil in a frying pan and brown lamb quickly on each side and on fat side also. Use tongs or two spoons for turning so that surface seal is not pierced. When browned but not cooked through, remove to a plate and leave until cold. Season lightly with salt. While lamb is cooling, soak apricots in sherry.

Melt butter in a clean pan and sauté onion until soft. Add curry powder and cook for a further minute. Remove to a bowl and add nuts, breadcrumbs, sugar, lemon rind and the soaked apricots. Mix well and season lightly with salt and pepper.

Lightly butter 2 fillo sheets together, butter top and fold in half. Brush top with butter. Place a chop 8 cm (3 inches) in from bottom edge of pastry with rib bone protruding 1 cm (½ inch) over the edge opposite the fold. Spread 2 scant tablespoons apricot mixture on top of the meat. Turn the folded side of the pastry onto the base of the chop, brush with butter then fold over short and long sides, tucking long end of pastry underneath the meat. (Lamb must be placed on the pastry so that there is sufficient length on one side to cover lamb and tuck underneath.) Twist the fillo pastry at the bone end around the rib bone. Place on a lightly greased baking sheet and brush top and sides of package with butter. Repeat with remaining ingredients.

Bake in a pre-heated moderately hot oven for 25 minutes for pink lamb. Once the oven has been turned off, the chops will survive a further 5 minutes if necessary — any longer and lamb will be well done. When serving, place a paper frill on end of each rib bone.

SEMOLINA CREAM ROLLS

Makes 8
Oven temperature
180-190°C (350-375°F)

These semolina cream-filled rolls, known as Bougatsa, are a speciality of Crete.

1¼ cups milk
½ cup fine semolina (cream of wheat)
⅓ cup sugar
pinch salt
2 eggs, beaten
½ teaspoon vanilla essence
8 sheets fillo pastry for Rolls I (page 27)
melted butter
cinnamon sugar for serving

In a heavy pan mix milk with semolina, sugar, salt and beaten eggs. Stir constantly over heat until very thick and paste-like. Any lumps can be stirred out with a balloon whisk early in cooking. Remove from heat, stir in vanilla essence and cover surface with plastic film. Leave until cold.

Butter a sheet of fillo, fold in half and butter top. Place about 3 tablespoons filling along one narrow edge about 4 cm (1½ inches) in from base and sides. Fold bottom edge of pastry loosely over filling, fold in sides and brush lightly with butter. Roll up loosely to end of sheet and place join side down onto lightly buttered baking sheet. Repeat with remaining

ingredients. Brush tops of rolls with butter and bake in a pre-heated moderately hot oven for 25 minutes until golden. Serve hot sprinkled with cinnamon sugar. Whipped cream may accompany the bougatsa.

BANANAS CALYPSO

Serves 6
Oven temperature
200-210°C (400-425°F)

6 medium-sized bananas, firm but ripe
60 g (2 oz) butter
¼ cup desiccated coconut
2 tablespoons brown sugar
1 tablespoon dark rum
6 sheets fillo pastry for Parcel I (page 28)
melted butter
FOR SERVING:
vanilla ice cream
Calypso Sauce with Rum (page 44)

Peel bananas and slit in half lengthwise. Place cut side down in a flat dish. Melt butter in a small pan, add coconut and heat, stirring occasionally, until coconut is golden — take care not to burn it. Remove from heat, stir in brown sugar and rum, and return to heat briefly to melt the sugar. Pour over bananas, leave a few minutes then turn bananas over and spread coconut mixture from dish over cut surface. Leave until mixture firms on bananas — refrigerate if necessary.

Brush a sheet of fillo with butter, fold in half and butter top. Place 2 banana halves across one corner and in from sides. Fold corner of pastry over banana, fold in sides and complete wrap. Place on a greased baking sheet, join side down, and brush with butter. Make similar parcels with remaining bananas and fillo. At this stage the completed parcels may be stored in the refrigerator, covered with foil, for up to 8 hours.

To bake, bring to room temperature for 1 hour if necessary and bake in a pre-heated hot oven for 10 minutes until golden brown. Serve hot with a scoop of vanilla ice cream on the side. Spoon hot Calypso Sauce with Rum over the ice cream at the table.

PINEAPPLE CARIBBEAN

Serves 6
Oven temperature
200-210°C (300-425°F)

1 small pineapple
freshly ground black pepper
2 tablespoons butter
1 tablespoon creme de cacao liqueur
6 sheets fillo pastry for Roll I (page 27)
melted butter
FOR SERVING:
vanilla ice cream
Calypso Sauce (page 44)

Peel pineapple and remove 'eyes'. Cut in half lengthwise, slice each half into 6 slender wedges along the length of the pineapple and cut out core. Spread out on a plate and dust lightly with freshly ground black pepper. Melt butter in a frying pan, add pineapple and cook on medium heat for 2 minutes, turning once. Pour liqueur over pineapple, ignite and shake pan until flames die down. Spoon pan liquid over pineapple and leave aside until cool. Turn pineapple occasionally.

Brush a sheet of fillo with butter and fold in half. Brush top with butter and overlap 2 pineapple wedges on pastry placing them towards narrow edge. Complete roll as directed and place join side down on a greased baking sheet. Make remaining rolls with pineapple and fillo. Store in refrigerator, covered with foil, at this stage if desired. They will hold for several hours or overnight.

To bake, bring rolls to room temperature for 1 hour if necessary and bake in a pre-heated hot oven for 10 minutes until golden brown. Serve hot with a scoop of vanilla ice cream on the side and pour hot Calypso Sauce over the ice cream at the table.

Note: Any pan juices remaining from the pineapple may be added to the sauce while it is boiling.

CALYPSO SAUCE

Makes about ¾ cup

1 tablespoon julienne shreds of
orange rind
water
2 tablespoons butter
½ cup brown sugar
⅓ cup orange juice
1 tablespoon lemon or lime juice
¼ cup creme de cacao liqueur

When preparing julienne shreds, peel rind from orange thinly using vegetable peeler so that very little pith remains on the rind. Cut into fine strips with a sharp knife. Place in a pan with cold water to cover and boil for 5 minutes. Rinse in cold water and drain. Keep aside.

Melt butter in a small pan and heat until golden brown. Remove pan from heat, add sugar and orange juice and stir well. Return to medium heat and bring to the boil. Add remaining ingredients and orange shreds and boil gently until syrupy — about 12-15 minutes. Cover pan and keep aside if not required immediately. Remove cover and return to the boil when required for serving. Pour hot sauce into a small jug and serve hot as directed in recipes.

Calypso Sauce with Rum Follow above recipe, replacing creme de cacao liqueur with 2 tablespoons dark rum or to taste. Amount depends on rum used.

Right: *Peaches 'n Cream with Sabayon Sauce (page 50).*

Overleaf, clockwise: *Seafood Amandine (page 54); Prawns Piraeus (page 34); Ginger Scallops (page 77) and Smoked Salmon Blintzes (page 31).*

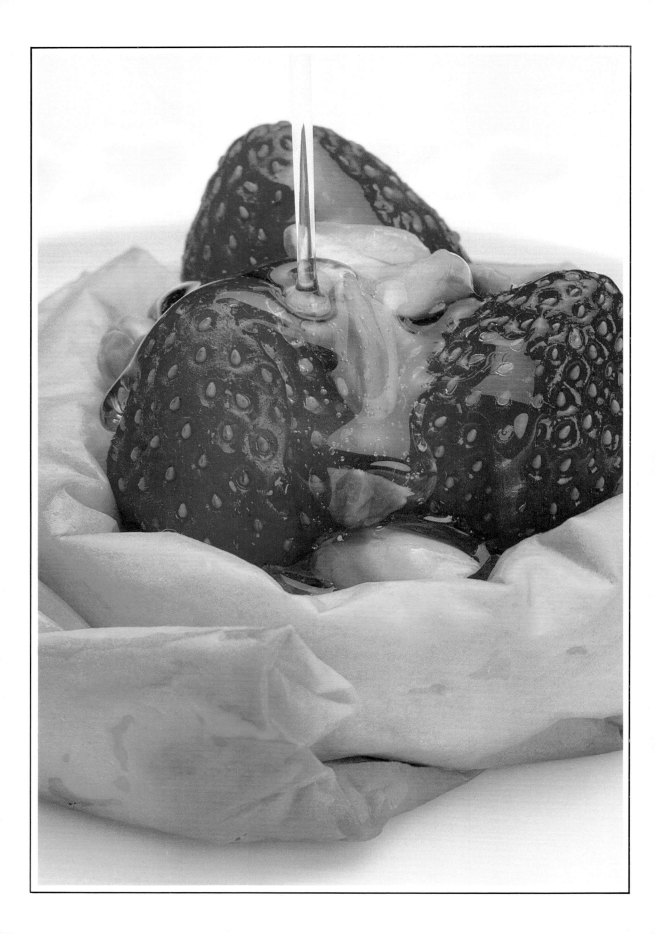

BIRD'S NEST PASTRIES

Makes 12
Oven temperature
170-180°C (325-350°F)

SYRUP:
1½ cups sugar
1 cup water
thin strip lemon rind
1 teaspoon lemon juice
1 teaspoon rose water
PASTRIES:
½ cup finely chopped blanched almonds
¼ cup finely chopped pistachio nuts
1 tablespoon caster sugar
12 sheets fillo pastry
melted butter or ghee
additional ¼ cup pistachio nuts,
coarsely chopped

Put sugar and water into a heavy pan and dissolve over heat, stirring occasionally. Add lemon rind and juice and bring to the boil. Boil, without stirring, for 12 minutes, add rose water, boil a few seconds then remove from heat and strain into a jug. Cool and chill in refrigerator.

When preparing nuts, it is preferable to chop with a knife or nut chopper — a food processor tends to over-chop them. Mix nuts with the tablespoon of sugar. Brush a sheet of fillo pastry with butter and fold in half across its width to give a long strip 15 cm (6 inches) wide. Brush again with butter and sprinkle 3 teaspoons nut mixture in a strip just above folded edge. Fold end of pastry over nuts, fold in 2 cm (¾ inch) of sides and roll up until a 4 cm (1½ inch) flap of pastry remains. Lift up roll so that flap hangs down, shape roll into a ring 8 cm (3 inches) in diameter overlapping ends. Tuck the loose flap of pastry into centre of ring to form base of nest and place on a buttered baking dish. Brush

Bird's Nest Pastries with Fruit (page 49).

completed pastries with melted butter and bake in a moderate oven for 20-25 minutes until golden and crisp. Pour half the cold syrup over the hot pastries and leave until cool. To serve, sprinkle 2 teaspoons coarsely chopped pistachio nuts in the centre of each pastry and place on dessert plates. Serve remainder of syrup in a small jug — float some small pink or red rose petals in the syrup for effect. Whipped cream may also accompany these pastries.

Bird's Nest Pastries with Fruit Make syrup as above, adding 1 tablespoon kirsch or rum in place of the rose water. Shape and bake pastries, pour on half the syrup. When serving, fill centre with strawberries, cooked apricot halves or fresh sliced peaches. Sprinkle a few nuts on top and serve with syrup and whipped cream served separately.

APPLE COILS

Makes about 12
Oven temperature
190-200°C (375-400°F)

410 g (15 oz) can unsweetened pie apple
¼ cup chopped seeded raisins
¼ cup caster sugar
½ teaspoon ground cinnamon
pinch ground cloves
¼ cup chopped almonds
12 sheets fillo pastry for Coils (page 27)
melted butter
2 tablespoons slivered or flaked almonds
for topping

Drain off any liquid from pie apple and place apple in a bowl. Mash with a fork to break up apple into small pieces. Mix in raisins, sugar, spices and almonds. Taste and add more sugar if necessary.

Butter a sheet of fillo pastry, fold, butter top, fill and shape as directed for shaping coils, using about 2 tablespoons filling for each coil. Place coils close together in a greased baking dish and brush tops with butter. Mix almonds with a little melted butter and sprinkle on top of coils. Bake in a pre-heated moderately hot oven for 20 minutes until crisp and golden. Serve hot with pouring cream if desired.

PEACHES 'N CREAM

Serves 6
Oven temperature
190-200°C (375-400°F)

3 large fresh peaches
1 cup ricotta cheese
½ cup chopped glacé fruits including
citrus peel
1 tablespoon kirsch
¼ cup chopped toasted almonds
6 or 12 sheets fillo pastry, depending
on thickness
melted butter
Sabayon Sauce for serving (page 50)

Peel peaches, halve and remove stones. Leave aside. Mix ricotta cheese with glacé fruits, kirsch and almonds.

Brush fillo sheet with butter. If fillo is very thin, top with another sheet and brush with butter. Fold in half across its length and lightly butter top. Place about 2 tablespoons of the ricotta mixture in a mound towards one corner of pastry. Lightly press a peach half on top of ricotta, rounded side up. Fold corner of pastry, fold sides over and brush folds with butter. Complete wrap so that peach is uppermost, tucking end of wrap underneath if necessary. Place on a greased baking sheet. Repeat with remaining ingredients. Brush tops and sides lightly with butter and bake in a pre-heated moderately hot oven for 15 minutes. Serve hot or warm with Sabayon Sauce served separately.

Alternative Wrapping Large squares of fillo sheets are required for this wrap. Fillo must be pliable — if fairly stiff do not attempt this wrap. Place 24 sheets pastry on a board and cut off excess length to give a square about 30 cm (12 inches). (The strips cut off may be re-wrapped and returned to the refrigerator, or used to make Cinnamon Sticks or Cheese Straws — see Index for recipes.) Cover squares with dry and damp cloths.

Take 4 squares and butter together, butter top and place cheese mixture and peach half in centre. Bring up the four corners of the pastry over the peach, hold gently with one hand, and with the other gather the fillo around the top of the peach. Press gently and tie a piece of string loosely around the pastry to hold it together. Bake as above, cut string with scissors and remove carefully. Garnish as desired.

SABAYON SAUCE

Makes about 1½ cups

Sabayon, a French version of the Italian Zabaglione, has to be served soon after it is made otherwise the mixture separates. However this version, once made, will survive for several hours, even overnight in the refrigerator — an advantage when entertaining and preparation beforehand is required. An electric hand mixer is preferable to using a hand beater as there is a lot of beating involved.

¾ cup sweet white wine
3 teaspoons cornflour
4 egg yolks
¼ cup caster sugar
1 tablespoon brandy

Place all but ¼ cup of the wine into a small pan and heat. Mix cornflour into remaining wine until smooth and pour into heating wine, stirring constantly. Keep stirring until thickened and bubbling. Boil gently for 1 minute and remove from heat.

Mix egg yolks with sugar in a heatproof bowl or the top of a double boiler (china or glass, not metal). Beat until creamy and place over simmering water. Beat in warmed thickened wine and continue to beat with a hand-held electric mixer until very thick and light. Beat for about 10-12 minutes, scraping down sides of bowl with a spatula to prevent egg cooking on the sides. Remove from heat and continue to beat for 1 minute, adding the brandy at this stage.

Pour into a serving jug or bowl and leave until cool, stirring gently now and then as it cools. Cover and leave at room temperature until required for serving, or store in the refrigerator overnight and bring to room temperature before serving.

THE BIG WRAP

A cloak of crisp, flaky pastry gives an air of mystery to the star of the main course. While fillo might not give the clean cut of puff pastry, you don't have the disadvantage of stodgy, uncooked dough. Preparation beforehand is the advantage — meat can be partly cooked, cooled, wrapped ready for baking and stored in the refrigerator.

When fillo was first marketed in Australia, it was labelled as Strudel Pastry. Now it is marketed in its own right; but it is excellent for strudels, though purists of strudel making do not agree. Strudel and fillo dough are basically the same — fillo differs only in its thickness. As a matter of fact, the first machine developed for making fillo pastry was based on a machine originally designed in Vienna for strudel pastry. Today the machines are made in Holland and the United States.

ENLARGED FILLO WRAP

Modern packaging has its limitations, so it is necessary in many instances to enlarge the size of the fillo wrap to enclose large food items adequately.

Clear a large area on which to work. Have fillo sheets opened out, stacked and covered with dry and damp cloths, as described on pages 7 to 8.

Brush 2 sheets fillo separately with melted butter and overlap about 12 cm (5 inches) of the longer edge of one sheet on top of the other to give a large squarish shape. Place another 2 sheets on top in the same manner and brush with butter. Continue to brush and overlap pastry using number of sheets specified in recipes — 6 or 8 sheets are usually sufficient for a large wrap. Recipes give directions for the placing of the food and method of wrapping. Always work with the completed wrap facing the same way as when assembled (see illustration overleaf), unless a recipe specifies otherwise.

Some recipes do not require the enlarged wrap. Fillo sheets are simply buttered and stacked. See Buttering Layers for details (page 69).

Decorating the Big Wrap

Beef Wellington, Lamb en Croute and similar dishes are frequently decorated with pastry strips and shapes. With fillo pastry, decorating with cut shapes is out of the question. However, it is possible to decorate with strips.

Cut a sheet of fillo pastry in half along its length. Fold up in 1 cm (½ inch) folds to give a thick strip of fillo. Make 2-4 such strips. After wrapped meat is placed on baking sheet and brushed with butter, place strips diagonally across the top. Tuck ends underneath the package and brush strips with butter.

About Strudels

Some strudel recipes require the enlarged wrap to ensure adequate enclosing of filling. Do not roll these strudels tightly as fillings expand during cooking. A true strudel is always rolled so that the completed roll is more oval than round, particularly when a soft filling is used.

Basically there are two techniques used for filling strudels. The more traditional method is to spread the filling over the wrap. As some of the pastry then ends up within the filling, it remains soft after cooking. When using fillo as the strudel pastry, it is preferable to place the filling towards one edge, so that all the pastry ends up around the filling, giving a thicker crust.

Dry fillings, such as in Walnut Strudel, are a different story. As the filling is usually loose, it can only be successfully wrapped if spread out and, because such fillings are drier, the pastry cooks within.

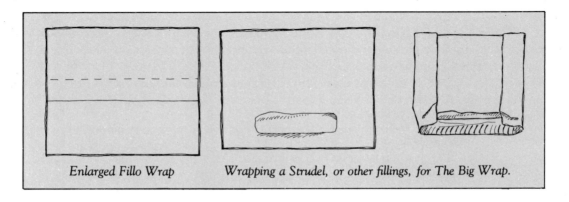

Enlarged Fillo Wrap   *Wrapping a Strudel, or other fillings, for The Big Wrap.*

VEGETARIAN DELIGHT

Serves 4-6
Oven temperature
180-190°C (350-375°F)

1 medium-sized eggplant
salt
2 tablespoons oil or butter
2 small onions, quartered and leaves
separated
1 cup red and green pepper pieces
1 cup thickly sliced zucchini
½ cup thinly sliced carrot
½ cup thinly sliced celery
¼ cup tomato paste
1 teaspoon brown sugar
½ teaspoon dried basil
2 tablespoons chopped parsley
1 tablespoon chopped celery leaves
freshly ground black pepper
½ cup soft wholemeal breadcrumbs
8 sheets fillo pastry for Enlarged
Wrap (page 51)
melted butter or substitute
2 tablespoons wheatgerm
1 tablespoon toasted sesame seeds
Cheese Sauce for serving (page 53)

Wash eggplant, leave skin on and cut into 2 cm (¾ inch) cubes. Place in a colander and sprinkle liberally with salt. Leave for 30 minutes, rinse and dry with absorbent paper. Heat half the oil in a pan, add eggplant and fry over fairly high heat, stirring often, until browned. Remove to a bowl. Add remaining oil to pan with onion, peppers, zucchini, carrot and celery. Stir over medium heat for 3 minutes until onion is transparent. Return eggplant to pan with tomato paste, sugar, herbs and add salt and pepper to taste. Toss lightly over medium heat until combined. Cover and cook for 10 minutes, remove lid and let excess moisture evaporate.

Make enlarged fillo wrap as directed. When 4 sheets have been buttered together brush top with butter and sprinkle with wheatgerm. Place remaining 4 sheets on top, buttering each sheet as it is put in place. Place wrap on a large tea towel.

Brush top with butter and sprinkle lower quarter of wrap with half the breadcrumbs, keeping 8 cm (3 inches) of sides clear of crumbs. Pile vegetable filling evenly in a band along centre of crumbs. Sprinkle top with breadcrumbs. Turn end of wrap over filling. Give roll a half turn using tea towel to facilitate rolling, and fold in sides. Complete roll and lift carefully onto a greased baking sheet, join side down. Cut 3 to 5 diagonal slashes along top of roll, spacing them evenly. Brush top and sides with butter and sprinkle sesame seeds on top.

Bake in a moderately hot oven for 20-25 minutes until golden. Serve cut into slices, using slashes in roll as a guide. Serve Cheese Sauce separately, to be poured on just before eating.

CHEESE SAUCE

Makes about 1¼ cups

1 tablespoon butter
1 tablespoon flour
1 cup milk
½ cup grated cheddar cheese
1 tablepoon grated parmesan cheese

Melt butter in a saucepan over low heat. Add flour and cook for 2-3 minutes. Remove from heat and add milk, stirring briskly. Bring to the boil, stirring constantly with a wooden spoon. Simmer 3 minutes then add grated cheese. Continue cooking over low heat until cheese has melted. If cooked for too long or over high heat after cheese has been added, the cheese may coagulate and separate.

SEAFOOD AMANDINE

Serves 6 as a first course, 4 as a main meal
Oven temperature
200-210°C (400-425°F)

250 g (8 oz) fish fillets (such as ling,
snapper or hake)
lemon juice
salt
freshly ground pepper
125 g (4 oz) fresh cleaned scallops
125 g (4 oz) cooked, shelled prawns
170 g (5½ oz) can crab meat
4 spring onions, chopped
2 teaspoons butter
SAUCE:
2 tablespoons butter
3 tablespoons flour
¾ cup milk
¼ cup cream
1 tablespoon lemon juice
TO FINISH:
8 sheets fillo pastry for Enlarged
Wrap (page 51)
melted butter
2 tablespoons slivered or flaked almonds
1 tablespoon lemon juice

Place fish fillets on a plate, sprinkle with lemon juice, salt and pepper and cover with another plate or foil. Place a trivet in a large pan and add water to come to top of trivet. Bring to the boil, place plate on trivet, cover pan and steam fish for 10-15 minutes until cooked — time depends on thickness of fish. Remove skin and bones from fish and flake flesh into large pieces. Place into a bowl with any liquid from plate. Add scallops, deveined prawns and crab meat. Sauté spring onions in butter and add to seafood. Cover and refrigerate until sauce is made.

To make the sauce, melt butter in a heavy pan, stir in flour and cook gently for 2 minutes. Pour in milk and cream, stirring constantly until thickened and bubbling. Season to taste and add lemon juice. Mix sauce gently into seafood, cover and leave in refrigerator to cool.

Make enlarged wrap as directed with fillo sheets and melted butter. Brush top with butter and place wrap on a tea towel. Place filling

towards bottom of wrap, 8 cm (4 inches) in from base and sides. Mound filling evenly, fold base and sides over filling and roll up, using tea towel to facilitate rolling. Place onto greased baking sheet, join side down and brush tops and sides with melted butter. Cut 3 or 5 diagonal slashes, evenly spaced, on top of roll.

Bake in a pre-heated hot oven for 20-25 minutes until golden. Lift carefully onto serving platter. Heat 2 tablespoons of the melted butter in a small pan, add the almonds and cook, stirring often, until golden brown. Pour in lemon juice and pour almonds immediately over roll. Slice through slashes in pastry when serving.
Note: This should be baked immediately after rolling filling in pastry. Filling can be pre-prepared and refrigerated.

KOULIBIAKA

Serves 6
Oven temperature
180-190°C (350-375°F)

425 g (15 oz) can red salmon
2 tablespoons butter
1½ cups chopped spring onions,
including some green tops
1½ cups sliced small mushrooms
1 tablespoon lemon juice
2 tablespoons chopped parsley
1½ teaspoons dried dill tips
1½ cups cooked rice (brown or white)
3 hard boiled eggs, chopped
salt and pepper to taste
12 sheets fillo pastry, see Buttering
Layers (page 69)
melted butter or substitute

Drain salmon, tip into bowl and remove skin and bones. Flake with a fork. Melt butter in a pan, add spring onions and fry gently for 2 minutes. Add mushrooms and 1 teaspoon of the lemon juice, stir and cook until mushrooms are limp. Add to salmon with remaining lemon juice, parsley, dill, rice and chopped eggs. Mix well and season to taste with salt and pepper.

Butter 6 sheets fillo pastry together in a stack as directed leaving top and bottom unbuttered.

Cover with a dry cloth. Butter another 6 sheets in a stack, brush top with butter and pile salmon mixture along the centre. Shape into a loaf about 10 cm (4 inches) wide and 25 cm (12 inches) long. Butter one side of the remaining stack of buttered sheets and place over the salmon loaf, buttered side down. Press pastry closely over loaf. Trim pastry so that an 8-10 cm (3-4 inch) border remains around loaf. Brush this border lightly with cold water and fold over border towards loaf using 1 cm (½ inch) folds. Do long sides first, brush folds at each end with water then fold up remaining sides. The water helps the fillo to stick in place.

Lift carefully onto lightly greased baking sheet. Brush top lightly with butter and make 5 evenly spaced shallow cuts along the top of the loaf. Bake in a moderate oven for 35 minutes until golden brown. Serve cut into slices using cuts in pastry as a guide. Serve hot with tartare sauce.

CHICKEN AND BROCCOLI ROLL

Serves 6
Oven temperature
200-210°C (400-425°F)

185 g (6 oz) broccoli florets
4 chopped spring onions
4 tablespoons butter
1 cup sliced small mushrooms
2 teaspoons lemon juice
2 cups cooked diced chicken
3 tablespoons flour
1½ cups chicken stock
¼ cup dry white wine
salt and white pepper
10 sheets fillo pastry for Englarged
Wrap (page 51)
melted butter or substitute
1 egg yolk
¼ cup cream

When cutting broccoli into small florets, leave some stem on. Par-boil in boiling salted water for 3 minutes, drain and refresh under cold water to arrest cooking. Drain well.

Sauté spring onions in 1 tablespoon butter until beginning to soften. Add mushrooms and lemon juice and cook until mushrooms are limp. Tip into a large bowl and add broccoli and chicken (cut in fairly large dice).

To make the sauce, melt remaining butter in a heavy pan, stir in flour and cook gently for 2 minutes. Pour in stock all at once, stirring constantly, then add wine. Keep stirring, bring to the boil and simmer gently for 3 minutes. Remove from heat. Add ½ cup of this sauce to the chicken mixture, fold through gently and season to taste with salt and pepper. Keep remaining sauce aside, covering surface with plastic film.

Using the 10 sheets fillo pastry and melted butter make an enlarged wrap as directed and place on a teatowel. Brush top of wrap with butter. Pile filling along one long edge of pastry leaving 10 cm (4 inches) of bottom and sides of wrap clear of filling. Fold bottom edge of pastry over filling and fold in sides. Brush folds with butter and roll up, lifting the tea towel to facilitate rolling. Place join side down on a lightly greased baking sheet. Lightly butter top and sides and make 5 evenly spaced diagonal slashes on top of the roll with a sharp knife. Bake in a pre-heated hot oven for 25 minutes until golden.

Towards end of cooking time for roll, complete the sauce. Return reserved sauce to heat and bring to a slow simmer, stirring often. Beat egg yolk with cream and stir into sauce. Heat gently, still stirring, until sauce begins to boil. Adjust seasoning. Serve roll sliced, with sauce served separately.

BEEF WELLINGTON

Serves 4-6
Oven temperature
190-200°C (375-400°F)

1 short fillet, about 800-900 g (1½-2 lbs)
freshly ground pepper
1 tablespoon butter
1 tablespoon oil
2 tablespoons brandy
additional tablespoon butter
¼ cup chopped spring onions
½ cup sliced small mushrooms
salt
6-8 sheets fillo pastry for Enlarged
Wrap (page 51)
melted butter or substitute
60 g pâté de fois
PORT SAUCE:
½ cup beef stock
¼ cup port
2 teaspoons cornflour mixed with
1 tablespoon water

The short fillet consists of 2 muscles, one bulging out on one side. Trim this back so that fillet is even in shape. Also remove visible silver skin and excess fat with a sharp knife. Your butcher might do this for you. Tie fillet at intervals with white string and season with pepper. Heat butter and oil in a frying pan and brown fillet on all sides, turning with blunt-ended tongs or two spoons. When brown, heat brandy gently in a ladle, ignite and pour flaming brandy over fillet. Spoon liquid in pan over fillet until flames die down. Remove fillet to a rack set on a dish and leave until cool. Reserve pan with drippings for sauce.

In a separate pan melt butter, add spring onions and cook for 1 minute. Add mushrooms and cook until juices evaporate. Keep aside. When meat is cold, remove string and dry with absorbent paper. Season lightly with salt.

Brush and stack fillo sheets as directed to make enlarged wrap. Brush top of wrap with butter and place fillet across one corner and in from edges of pastry. Spread top with pâté and press onion-mushroom mixture onto pâté. Bring corner of pastry over the meat, roll once then fold in sides. Brush side folds with butter and roll to end. The pâté mixture should be on

top when wrapping is complete. Place join side down (trimmed back if necessary) on lightly greased baking sheet. Brush top and sides lightly with butter and bake in a pre-heated moderately hot oven for 30 minutes for rare, 35 minutes for medium rare. (End pieces will be cooked a little more for those who prefer meat medium done.) Remove to warm serving platter and leave 5-10 minutes before carving. Serve Port Sauce separately.

Port Sauce (Make while meat is 'resting'). Pour stock and port into pan used for browning fillet, place over heat and stir well to dissolve juices. Stir in cornflour and water paste and bring to the boil. Boil gently for 1 minute and adjust seasoning. Strain into a sauceboat. A little cream or butter may be stirred into the sauce at the end of cooking.

BEEF COBBLER

Serves 4-5
Oven temperature
200-210°C (400-425°F)

2 tablespoons chopped bacon
1 tablespoon butter
1 large onion, chopped
1 clove garlic, crushed
500 g (1 lb) finely ground beef
1 cup sliced small mushrooms
2 tablespoons flour
½ cup beef stock
¼ cup dry red wine
1 tablespoon tomato paste
salt
freshly ground black pepper
½ teaspoon sugar
2 tablespoons chopped parsley
¼ teaspoon powdered thyme leaves
8 sheets fillo pastry
melted butter or substitute

Put bacon into a heated pan and cook until fat renders. Add butter and onion and cook gently until onion is soft. Add garlic, then ground beef and increase heat. Stir often to break up lumps, adding mushrooms after meat changes colour. Cook until juices evaporate and sprinkle in flour. Stir over heat for 2 minutes and stir in stock, wine and tomato paste. Reduce heat, add salt and pepper to taste, sugar and herbs. Cover and simmer gently for 10 minutes. Leave until cool.

Butter and stack fillo pastry sheets. Brush top with butter and pile cold meat filling along bottom edge of pastry, 8-10 cm (3-4 inches) in from sides and base of wrap. Turn bottom edge of pastry loosely over filling, give roll a half turn, folding over as loosely as possible, turn again, then fold in sides. Complete roll and lift onto greased baking sheet. Brush top and sides with butter and cut 3 or 4 diagonal slashes along top of roll, according to number of serves. Bake in a pre-heated hot oven for 25 minutes.

Note: While it takes a little more effort to prepare, the enlarged wrap detailed on page 51 encloses the Cobbler more effectively. With the normal wrap, the roll might burst its sides a little, but still gives an acceptable result. I have also wrapped the filling in small parcels to give individual serves. The filling makes 6-7 parcels, each containing about 4 tablespoons of filling. See directions for Parcel I (page 28). If making the smaller parcels, you will need 12-14 fillo sheets.

LAMB LOIN EN CROUTE

Serves 4-5
Oven temperature
180-190°C (350-375°F)

1 boned mid loin of lamb, about
1 kg (2 lb) after boning
juice of ½ lemon
salt and pepper
8 sheets fillo pastry for Enlarged
Wrap (page 51)

SPINACH AND PINE NUT STUFFING:
2 tablespoons butter
2 tablespoons pine nuts
1 small onion, finely chopped
1 clove garlic, crushed
250 g (8 oz) packet frozen leaf
spinach, thawed
2 tablespoons breadcrumbs
salt and pepper
pinch ground nutmeg

When purchasing lamb loin, ensure that a longish flap is retained on the loin so that filling may be enclosed. Have butcher bone the lamb.

Pull off fine skin covering fat on loin and, if necessary, trim fat carefully so that a thin covering remains. Rub all over with lemon juice and season inside the loin with salt and pepper.

To prepare the stuffing, melt half the butter in a frying pan, add pine nuts and cook on medium heat until golden. Remove with draining spoon to a bowl, leaving butter in pan. Add onion to pan with remaining butter, fry gently until transparent, add garlic and cook a few seconds. Add to pine nuts. Drain spinach well, pressing out excess moisture and chop roughly. Add to pine nuts with crumbs, salt and pepper to taste and a good pinch ground nutmeg. Mix well.

Place stuffing along inside of loin, roll up and secure roll with poultry skewers. Tie firmly at intervals and remove skewers. Rub with salt and pepper. Grease a large heated frying pan with a little trimmed lamb fat and slowly brown loin on medium heat on all sides. Lamb should take about 25-30 minutes to brown. When browned remove to a plate and leave until completely cold. Remove all strings except for those at each end.

Make enlarged wrap as directed with the fillo sheets and melted butter. Wipe lamb with absorbent paper and place loin towards one corner of the wrap. Fold corner of wrap over the lamb, fold in sides and brush folds with butter. Complete the wrap and place join side down onto a lightly greased baking sheet. Brush top and sides with melted butter. Decorate with pastry strips if desired (see page 51). Bake in a pre-heated moderately hot oven for 30 minutes. Allow lamb to stand in a warm place for 5-10 minutes before carving. Serve carved in thick slices.

Note: I prefer spinach for this dish, and frozen leaf spinach is as good as fresh spinach and more convenient. If leaf spinach is not available do not use chopped spinach as it is too fine. Instead use fresh spinach, washed well, heated in a pan until wilted and drained well. Silverbeet (Swiss Chard) is often used in place of spinach — I do not consider it a good substitute in this recipe.

PORK GLEN HUON

Serves 4
Oven temperature
190-200°C (375-400°F)

½ cup dried apricot halves
½ cup apple cider
1 small cooking apple
grated rind of 1 lemon
2 tablespoons chopped, toasted hazelnuts
2 pork fillets, each about 300 g (10 oz)
1 tablespoon butter
freshly ground black pepper
salt
6 sheets fillo pastry for Enlarged
Wrap (page 51)
melted butter
APRICOT CIDER SAUCE:
3 teaspoons flour
¼ cup apple cider
reserved puréed apricots
¼ cup water
1 teaspoon French mustard
2 tablespoons port
1 teaspoon sugar
¼ cup cream

Place apricots in a small pan with the apple cider. Bring slowly to the boil and simmer gently, covered, for 15 minutes or until apricots are plump but still intact. Drain in a sieve set over a bowl. Put all but 5 apricot halves into another bowl. Purée the 5 apricots with the cooking liquid and reserve for sauce later.

Peel apple, halve and core. Cut into slender wedges. Add to drained apricots with lemon rind and hazelnuts. Toss lightly to mix.

Trim any gristle and fat from the pork fillets. Cut a long, deep slash in each fillet beginning and ending 3 cm (1¼ inches) from each end. Open out fillets — they will look like long canoes. Fill with apricot-apple mixture and place fillets so that thin tail of one is adjacent to thick end of the other. Carefully turn one filled fillet (still opened) on top of the other to give a thick, even shape. Tie fillets together in several places with white string and tie across their length folding the thin end of the fillet over the thick end at each end of roll. If filling shows, push it in and if necessary close any gaps with poultry pins. Season pork with pepper.

Heat butter in a large frying pan until foaming. Place pork in pan and brown on all sides over medium heat, turning often with tongs or 2 spoons. Cook for 15 minutes altogether. Remove to a plate and leave until cold. Drain any juices back into pan and keep pan aside for making sauce.

Make enlarged wrap as directed with fillo sheets and melted butter. Brush top with butter. Dry pork with paper towels, season lightly with salt and remove poultry pins and string. Handle carefully once untied so it does not fall apart.

Place pork towards one end of wrap, fold end over pork and fold in sides. Complete wrap, but do not wrap too tightly. Place join side down onto a greased baking sheet. Brush top with butter and, if desired, decorate roll with fillo pastry strips (see page 51) and brush with butter. Pork can be stored, covered, in refrigerator until needed. Bring to room temperature 1 hour before baking.

Bake in a preheated moderately hot oven for 20-25 minutes until golden. Serve cut in thick slices, or cut roll diagonally into 4 pieces. Serve Apricot Cider Sauce separately.

Apricot Cider Sauce Place pan in which pork has been browned over heat and leave until moisture evaporates. Add a little more butter if necessary and stir in flour. Cook a minute on medium heat, then stir in cider, reserved apricot purée and water. Browned sediment in pan will give the necessary stock flavour. Stir until thickened and bubbling and add mustard, port and sugar. Season to taste and stir in cream. Heat gently and thin down if necessary with apple cider. Pour into a sauce boat.

LAMB LOIN WITH CHERRY STUFFING

Serves 6
Oven temperature
190-200°C (375-400°F)

1 boned mid loin of lamb,
about 1 kg (2 lb) after boning
salt and pepper
8 sheets fillo pastry for Enlarged
Wrap (page 51)
melted butter

CHERRY STUFFING:
1 small onion, finely chopped
1 tablespoon butter
1 cup soft breadcrumbs
grated rind of 1 lemon
¾ cup drained, bottled morello
cherries, pitted
¼ teaspoon ground cinnamon
1 small egg, beaten

CHERRY SAUCE:
½ cup liquid from cherries
¼ cup light stock
2 teaspoons cornflour
¼ cup port
pinch ground cinnamon
1 teaspoon sugar

Ask for a loin with a long flap so that filling may be enclosed. Pull off fine skin covering fat on loin and, if necessary, trim fat carefully so that only a thin covering remains. Season inside of loin lightly with salt and pepper and spread out flat, fat side down.

To prepare the stuffing, in a frying pan gently cook onion in butter until soft. Tip butter and onion into a bowl and add crumbs, lemon rind, well-drained cherries and cinnamon. Season lightly with salt and pepper and add enough beaten egg to bind (about 1½ tablespoons). Place stuffing along the centre of the loin and skewer into a neat roll. Tie at intervals with white string and remove skewers. Tie around the length of the loin.

Heat a large greased frying pan and brown loin slowly on all sides — this takes about 25-30 minutes. Remove to a dish and leave until cold. Drain fat from pan and keep pan aside for making sauce. When loin is completely cold remove all strings except those tied at each end.

With fillo sheets and melted butter assemble large wrap as directed and lightly butter top. Place cold lamb across one corner of the wrap and in from the sides. Fold corner over lamb, fold in sides and brush folds with butter. Roll to end of sheet. Place join side down onto lightly greased baking sheet and brush top and sides with butter. Bake in a preheated moderately hot oven for 30 minutes. Let it stand 5-10 minutes before carving. Serve hot with the Cherry Sauce served separately.

Cherry Sauce To pan in which lamb was browned, add cherry liquid and stock. Stir over heat to dissolve browned sediment. Mix cornflour with port and gradually pour into pan, stirring constantly until thickened and bubbling. Add cinnamon and sugar and season to taste if necessary. Strain into a sauce boat.

WALNUT STRUDEL

Makes 10-12 slices
Oven temperature
180-190°C (350-375°F)

½ cup soft breadcrumbs
1 tablespoon butter
2 cups coarsely ground walnuts
1 cup sultanas
grated rind of 1 lemon
⅓ cup brown sugar
1 teaspoon vanilla essence
6 sheets fillo pastry, see Buttering
Layers (page 69)
melted butter or substitute
icing sugar for serving

Place breadcrumbs and butter in a heavy frying pan over medium heat and stir well to distribute butter. Cook, stirring often, until crumbs are crisp and browned lightly. Place crumbs in a bowl with walnuts, sultanas, lemon rind, sugar and vanilla essence and mix well.

Butter fillo sheets together in a stack and brush top with butter. Sprinkle bottom half of pastry with walnut mixture, keeping 4-8 cm (1½-3 inches) in from sides. Dribble 2 tablespoons of the melted butter over the filling. Fold sides in and roll up firmly. Place join side down onto a lightly buttered baking sheet. Brush top and sides lightly with butter. Using a sharp knife, make diagonal slashes 3 cm (1¼ inches) apart on the top of the roll.

Bake in a pre-heated moderate oven for 35-40 minutes until golden. Leave on baking sheet to cool a little and sprinkle with sifted icing sugar. Serve cut into diagonal slices using slashes as guide. Lightly sweetened whipped cream flavoured with vanilla essence is excellent served with this strudel.

CHERRY CHEESE STRUDEL

Makes 8 slices
Oven temperature
180-190°C (350-375°F)

425 g (15 oz) can black pitted cherries
1 cup ricotta cheese
1 egg yolk
¼ cup caster sugar
grated rind of ½ lemon
2 tablespoons butter
½ cup soft breadcrumbs
¼ cup flaked almonds
½ teaspoon ground cinnamon
6 sheets fillo pastry, see Buttering
Layers (see page 69)
melted butter
TOPPING:
1 tablespoon flaked almonds
cinnamon sugar, optional
CHERRY SAUCE (optional):
¾ cup syrup from cherries
1 small cinnamon stick
2 teaspoons kirsch
2 teaspoons arrowroot
2 tablespoons water

Drain cherries, reserving liquid. Place cherries on absorbent paper to drain thoroughly. In a bowl mix ricotta with egg yolk, sugar and lemon rind. Melt the 2 tablespoons butter in a small saucepan, add breadcrumbs and almonds and stir occasionally over heat until crumbs and almonds are golden. Remove from heat and add cinnamon.

Layer fillo sheets with melted butter as directed, following Stack or Book method. Place stack on a tea towel. Brush top with butter and sprinkle half the browned crumb mixture evenly on lower third of pastry, keeping 6-10 cm (2½-4 inches) of sides clear. Put the cheese mixture along the centre of the crumbs and shape it evenly with a spatula. Place drained cherries along centre of cheese and sprinkle remaining crumb mixture on top. Using tea towel, lift base of pastry over filling. Fold in sides and roll to end of sheet. Cherries should be uppermost when roll is complete, so trim off excess pastry if necessary. Place join

side down on a greased baking sheet and cut 7 evenly spaced diagonal slashes along top. Mix about 2 teaspoons melted butter with the 1 tablespoon flaked almonds and spread on top of the strudel. Sprinkle lightly with cinnamon sugar and bake in a pre-heated moderate oven one shelf above centre, for 20 minutes. Serve warm with Cherry Sauce or whipped cream.

Cherry Sauce Put syrup into a small pan with cinnamon stick and simmer gently for 10 minutes. Remove cinnamon and add kirsch to syrup. Mix arrowroot with water and gradually stir into simmering syrup, stirring constantly. Let sauce boil gently for 1 minute and remove from heat. Allow the sauce to cool, stirring occasionally to prevent a skin forming on top. Serve warm or cold in a small sauce jug.

APPLE STRUDEL

Makes 8 slices
Oven temperature
180-190°C (350-375°F)

Apple Strudel is usually made with raw apple, but I have it on good authority that cooked apple should be used. With fillo pastry, cooked apple gives a much better result.

410 g (15 oz) can unsweetened pie apple
¼ cup caster sugar
¼ teaspoon vanilla essence
½ teaspoon ground cinnamon
½ cup sultanas (white raisins)
grated rind of 1 lemon
½ cup soft breadcrumbs
½ cup chopped walnuts or pecans
8 sheets fillo pastry for Enlarged
Wrap (page 51)
melted butter or substitute
icing sugar for serving

Drain pie apple if necessary and place in a bowl. Add sugar, vanilla essence, cinnamon, sultanas and grated lemon rind. Combine thoroughly.

Make enlarged wrap with the fillo pastry and melted butter as directed and brush top of stack with butter. Sprinkle bottom half of pastry with half of the breadcrumbs leaving 8-10 cm (3-4 inches) of sides clear, depending on size of sheet. Sprinkle half of the nuts on top. Place apple mixture in a rounded strip along the centre of the crumbs and nuts and sprinkle remaining crumbs and nuts on top.

Fold end nearest you over the apple mixture and fold in sides. Brush side folds with melted butter and roll up to end. Place join side down on lightly greased baking sheet and brush top and sides with butter. Cut diagonal slashes in pastry 4 cm (1½ inches) apart. Bake in a pre-heated moderately hot oven for 35-40 minutes. Just before serving sift some icing sugar on top. Cut in slices using slashes in pastry as a guide. This strudel is at its best served warm. Whipped cream, lightly sweetened and flavoured with vanilla essence, should be served separately.

PLUM STRUDEL BRAID

Makes 6-8 slices
Oven temperature
190-200°C (375-400°F)

Soft, pliable fillo sheets need to be used for this strudel, otherwise you may have difficulty when braiding it. If the fillo is fairly stiff, then make an ordinary rolled strudel with the filling. Make an enlarged wrap (page 51) using 8 sheets fillo, and finish with the crumb and almond topping. Bake for 30-35 minutes.

2 tablespoons butter
2 cups soft breadcrumbs
820 g (30 oz) can dark plums in syrup
½ teaspoon ground cinnamon
2 tablespoons brown sugar
grated rind of 1 lemon
12 sheets fillo pastry, see Buttering Layers (page 69)
additional teaspoon brown sugar
1 tablespoon flaked almonds
icing sugar
Plum Sauce or Cinnamon Cream, see directions at end of recipe

Melt butter in a heavy frying pan, add crumbs and stir well to distribute butter. Leave on medium heat and stir often until lightly browned and crisp. Remove 2 tablespoons crumbs and keep aside.

Drain plums well, reserving syrup. Remove seeds and place plums into a bowl. Add crumbs from pan, cinnamon, sugar and lemon rind and mix well.

Butter together fillo sheets in 3 stacks of 4 sheets each, leaving top and bottom of stacks unbuttered. Cover two of the stacks with dry, then damp cloths. Have ready a lightly buttered baking sheet which is about the same length as the fillo.

Butter top of one stack of fillo and with longer edge facing you, place a third of the plum mixture (about ⅔ cup) in a thick band towards bottom edge and 4-6 cm (1½-2½ inches) in from sides. Roll up fairly loosely into a roll. Place roll join side down along the centre of the baking sheet. Make another 2 rolls in the same way, placing them on either side of the first roll. Braid (or plait) the three rolls and tuck ends underneath. Brush top and sides of braid with butter.

Mix the teaspoon brown sugar with the reserved crumbs and sprinkle on top of the braid. Mix flaked almonds with a little melted butter and sprinkle on top of crumbs. Bake in a pre-heated moderately hot oven for 20-25 minutes.

Sift icing sugar lightly on top and serve strudel hot or warm cut into thick slices. Serve Plum Sauce or Cinnamon Cream separately.

Plum Sauce Mix 4 teaspoons arrowroot with ¼ cup plum syrup. Bring remaining syrup to the boil with a small piece of cinnamon stick and boil for 5 minutes. Remove from heat and stir in arrowroot mixture. Return to heat and stir constantly until thickened and bubbling. Remove cinnamon stick and serve hot or warm.

Cinnamon Cream Whip 1 cup cream until soft peaks form. Fold in 1 tablespoon caster sugar and ¼ teaspoon ground cinnamon.

APRICOT PUFF

Makes 6-8 slices
Oven temperature
180-190°C (350-375°F)

1½ cups dried apricots
1 cup hot water
¼ cup sugar
thin strip lemon rind
¼ teaspoon ground cinnamon
12 sheets fillo pastry, see Buttering
Layers (page 69)
melted butter
icing sugar

Rinse apricots if necessary. Place in a saucepan with the hot water and leave to soak for 15 minutes. Add sugar and lemon rind and bring slowly to the boil. Cover and simmer on low heat for 30-40 minutes until apricots are plump and most of syrup is absorbed. Take care that apricots do not burn. Remove lemon rind, leave apricots until cold and drain off excess syrup. Mix cinnamon lightly into apricots.

Stack the 12 fillo sheets and measure length. If longer than 40 cm (16 inches) cut off excess. Butter the stack of fillo following Book Method (page 70), leaving top of stack unbuttered. Cut in half across its length to give 2 rectangular stacks 20 cm (8 inches) wide.

Butter the centre of both stacks of fillo, leaving a 3 cm (1¼ inch) border unbuttered. Spread apricots evenly over the buttered section on one stack and brush the unbuttered border lightly with water. Invert second stack on top of the apricots, buttered side down. Press edges around apricots to seal, and trim outer edges with a sharp knife if necessary so that they are even. The finished pastry will be flat, mounding slightly over the apricots.

Place on a greased baking sheet and brush top lightly with butter. Score fillo over the apricot section only, making a shallow cut down the centre along the length of the pastry, and 2 or 3 shallow cuts across the width, dividing it into 6 or 8 portions. Sprinkle top lightly with water.

Bake in a pre-heated moderate oven for 30-35 minutes until flaky and golden brown. Cool on baking sheet and dust top with sifted icing sugar. Cut into portions using slashes as a guide

and serve warm as a dessert with pouring or whipped cream, or cold as a pastry with whipped cream.

Note: A fan-forced oven can cause the pastry to flake unevenly. To prevent this, place the pastry in a greased baking dish and place dish on shelf just above fan. If your oven has variable speeds, use slow fan setting.

BANANA DATE ROLL

Makes 6 slices
Oven temperature
180-190°C (350-375°F)

6 small bananas, ripe but firm
3 teaspoons lemon juice
½ cup chopped dates
2 tablespoons chopped cashew nuts
or walnuts
2 tablespoons brown sugar
¼ teaspoon ground cinnamon
2 tablespoons melted butter
8 sheets fillo pastry for Enlarged
Wrap (page 51)
melted butter
cinnamon sugar

Peel bananas and halve lengthwise. Spread out on a plate cut side up, and sprinkle with lemon juice. Mix dates with nuts, brown sugar, cinnamon and 1 tablespoon melted butter.

Make enlarged wrap as directed with fillo sheets and brush top with butter. Place 6 of the banana halves, cut side up, in 2 rows 8 cm (3 inches) in from base and sides of wrap, and with bananas parallel to base. Spread date mixture evenly on top of the bananas, then place remaining bananas on top, cut side down. Dribble remaining tablespoon butter over filling. Fold base of wrap over filling, turn once then fold in sides and brush side folds with butter. Roll up to end of wrap.

Place join side down on a greased baking sheet and brush top and sides of roll with butter. Cut 5 evenly spaced diagonal slashes on the top of the roll and dust lightly with cinnamon sugar.

Bake in a pre-heated moderate oven for 35-40 minutes until golden. Serve hot or warm with stirred custard or pouring cream.

POPPY SEED STRUDEL

Makes about 12 slices
Oven temperature
180-190°C (350-375°F)

If you like poppy seeds, then you should like this strudel. Poppy seeds have a nutty flavour, but it must be released by grinding the seeds, or steaming them. Few cookbooks have recipes for this popular Hungarian strudel and it is included for poppy seed lovers. While these slate-blue coloured seeds come from the opium poppy, the seed has no narcotic properties.

1 cup poppy seeds
⅓ cup sugar
½ cup sultanas or chopped seeded raisins, optional
grated rind of 1 lemon
2 tablespoons sour cream
5 sheets fillo pastry, see Buttering Layers (page 69)
melted butter or substitute
additional tablespoon poppy seeds
icing sugar for serving

Grind poppy seeds in a blender, a ¼ cup at a time, just long enough to crack them. If you purchase poppy seeds ready ground (sometimes available), you will require 1¼ cups ground seeds. Place ground seeds in a bowl and add sugar, sultanas if used, lemon rind and sour cream. Mix well until combined.

Butter and stack fillo sheets. Brush top with butter and spread poppy seed mixture over bottom half of pastry, keeping 6-10 cm (2½-4 inches) of sides clear of filling. (Border at sides depends on length of fillo sheet.) Fold in sides over filling and brush folds with butter. Roll up firmly and place join side down onto greased baking sheet. Brush top and sides with butter and cut shallow, diagonal slashes 2.5 cm (1 inch) apart across top of strudel. Sprinkle with poppy seeds if desired and bake in a pre-heated moderate oven for 30-35 minutes until golden. Take care not to overcook it as poppy seeds could burn. Cool on baking sheet and sift icing sugar onto warm roll. Serve warm or cold cut into slices, using slashes in pastry as a guide.

ROLLED BAKLAVA

Makes 18 slices
Oven temperature
150-160°C (300-325°F)

1 cup finely chopped walnuts
1 cup finely chopped almonds
1 large egg white
¼ cup caster sugar
1 teaspoon ground cinnamon
pinch ground cloves
8 sheets fillo, see Buttering Layers (page 69)
melted butter
SYRUP:
1 cup sugar
¾ cup water
thin strip lemon rind
1 tablespoon lemon juice
small piece cinnamon stick

Prepare nuts in food processor with steel blade, but stop processing as soon as nuts are finely chopped — some will be ground but this is acceptable. Do them separately as the walnuts tend to chop up more quickly than the almonds.

Beat egg white until stiff and beat in sugar gradually. Fold in nuts, cinnamon and cloves.

Butter and stack the 8 sheets of fillo, butter top and place stack with the short side towards you. Cover three quarters of the fillo with the nut mixture, working away from you, leaving the furthest quarter clear of filling. Roll up as for Swiss or Jelly Roll, beginning at nut-filled end. Finish with join side underneath. Cut roll into slices approximately 1.5 cm (½ inch) wide and place on a lightly greased baking dish. Brush tops and sides with butter. Bake in a moderately slow oven for 40 minutes.

Make the syrup by dissolving the sugar in the water over heat. Add lemon rind, juice and cinnamon stick and bring to the boil. Boil without stirring for 12 minutes or until a thin honey consistency. Strain and cool. Pour cooled syrup over hot pastries. Serve when cool and store at room temperature in a sealed container.

DRIED FRUIT STRUDEL

Makes about 12 slices
Oven temperature
180-190°C (350-375°F)

½ cup seeded raisins
½ cup chopped dates
4 dessert figs, chopped
¼ cup glacé cherries
½ cup chopped walnuts or pecans
½ cup ground almonds
½ teaspoon ground cinnamon
grated rind of 1 lemon
2 tablespoons caster sugar
2 tablespoons melted butter
6 sheets fillo pastry, see Buttering
Layers (page 69)
melted butter or substitute
icing sugar for serving

Prepare dried fruits and nuts and place in a bowl. Add cinnamon, lemon rind, sugar and the 2 tablespoons melted butter. Mix well to combine.

Butter fillo sheets together following Stack or Book method. Brush top with butter. Spread fruit mixture over pastry, leaving a 6 cm (2½ inch) border of pastry clear of filling. Turn one long end of pastry over filling and fold in sides. Brush side folds with butter and roll up firmly.

Place join side down on a lightly greased baking sheet. Cut diagonal slashes along the top, spacing them about 3 cm (1¼ inches) apart. Brush top with butter and bake in a preheated moderate oven for 30-35 minutes until golden. Cool on tray and dust with sifted icing sugar.

To serve, cut into slices using slashes in pastry as a guide. This strudel keeps for a week or so, stored in a sealed container at room temperature.

CHEESE STRUDEL

Makes 8 slices
Oven temperature
180-190°C (350-375°F)

1½ cups ricotta cheese
¼ cup caster sugar
¼ cup sultanas
grated rind of 1 lemon
½ teaspoon vanilla essence
2 egg yolks
6 sheets fillo pastry, see Buttering
Layers (see page 69)
melted butter
½ cup soft bread or cake crumbs
ground cinnamon
1 tablespoon ground almonds, optional
cinnamon sugar or icing sugar

Soften ricotta cheese in a bowl using a wooden spoon and mix in caster sugar, sultanas, lemon rind, vanilla and egg yolks. Keep aside.

Layer fillo sheets with melted butter, following Stack or Book methods. Brush top with melted butter and sprinkle half the crumbs along the bottom third of the pastry, keeping 6-10 cm (2½-4 inches) of sides clear. Sprinkle lightly with cinnamon and place cheese mixture on top in a thick strip, about 30 cm (12 inches) long. Top with remaining crumbs and a little cinnamon. Turn base of pastry over filling, fold in sides and roll loosely to end of sheet. Place join side down on a greased baking sheet and brush top and sides with butter. Cut diagonal slashes along top, spacing them 4-5 cm (1½-2 inches) apart. Sprinkle on ground almonds and cinnamon sugar or leave plain. Bake in a pre-heated moderate oven, one shelf above centre, for 20 minutes. If almond topping is not used, sprinkle with icing sugar. Serve warm cut in slices.

Right: *Plum Strudel Braid (page 61).*
Overleaf: *Bagged Carpetbag Steaks (page 41) and Beef Wellington (page 56).*

PIES AND TARTS

A fillo crusted pie is not your usual round or oval creation, though it can be used for traditional shapes. In Greek cuisine, pies are *large,* baked in a Greek round baking dish called a tapsi (at least 30 cm or 12 inches in diameter) or in the rectangular baking dish familiar to most cooks. Of the sweet pies or pastries, baklava is probably the best known and as you will see, there is more than one way to make a Baklava.

Fillo pastry can replace puff and shortcrust pastry to a certain extent. As a pastry base for a flan or tart it is best baked without a filling, with the hot filling added just before serving. Remember it is a delicate pastry which was certainly not intended for dishes such as quiche. However a quiche-type filling may be used providing there is a top crust so that you can fully appreciate the delicate fillo.

The principal technique is to layer a number of fillo sheets with melted butter or oil brushed on each sheet. Usually sheets are placed one by one into the dish, then brushed while in the dish. This can be time-consuming, so try either of these methods for buttering or oiling fillo sheets when a number of sheets are required for pies etc. I call one the Stack Method, as you work with the sheets in a stack. As you are constantly turning the sheets, the fillo has little chance of drying out. The second method is the Book Method, a good method for very fine fillo sheets, which keeps the pastry sheets neatly together and also gives the fillo less opportunity to dry.

For large pies choose a dish which will give you minimum wastage of fillo. As some manufacturers make sheets which are longer than the dimensions of standard baking dishes, this might not be possible. However there is no need to waste the fillo. Place dish on top of the stack of fillo, allow for sides of dish, then cut off excess on one side while stacked. Using Pastry Strips (page 70) will tell you how to use them.

BUTTERING LAYERS OF FILLO SHEETS

Stack Method

Place required number of fillo sheets in a stack on a flat surface, covering remaining sheets with dry then damp cloths. Stack should be placed on a flat work surface with longer edge towards you. Brush top sheet of stack with butter or oil. Lift sheet from the two top or two bottom corners and turn sheet upside down onto stack. Do not be concerned if sheet wrinkles a little — just smooth out with hand. Butter again, lift the two top sheets and turn upside down. Keep buttering and turning, lifting an extra sheet each time. Leave top and bottom of stack unbuttered. Pastry edges might be uneven — these can be trimmed later. Lift into greased dish, or use as directed in recipes.

Creamed Mushroom Tarts (page 75).

Book Method

Place required number of fillo sheets in a stack on a flat surface and fold in half so that stack is like a closed book. Turn top sheet over onto surface and brush with butter. Turn next sheet, butter, and so on until the top of the stack is reached. Leave top unbuttered and fold again in the opposite direction. Open sheets one by one and butter. Leave top unbuttered. Lift into dish or cut into squares for certain recipes.

Using Pastry Strips

If using the Stack Method of buttering, after 2 sheets are buttered together, butter top of stack and place strips side by side to cover buttered sheet. Butter top, proceed with stack, every now and then placing strips onto buttered top. A strip layer is counted as a fillo sheet so take these layers into account when counting your sheets. However an extra sheet or two will not affect your recipe. Many uses for pastry strips may be found in the chapter on Little Wrap-ups.

Cutting and Scoring into Diamonds

Baklavas and other Greek-style pies call for cutting or scoring the completed pie into diamond or lozenge shapes. Trim edges of fillo evenly with top of dish and score or cut in evenly spaced lines along the length of the pie; the closer the lines, the smaller the final pieces will be. Now score or cut diagonally across the pie, with lines spaced the same as the vertical lines, (see illustration page 71). Only cut or score surface of pie, not the edges. Use a Stanley knife or scalpel for trimming and scoring, a sharp, pointed knife for cutting. Sprinkle buttered top lightly with cold water to prevent pastry curling during cooking.

Fan-forced Ovens and Fillo

For owners of fan-forced (convection) ovens, baklava for example can be a problem as the fan can cause the pastry to flake unevenly at the sides and sometimes causes displacement of the top layers.

To overcome this problem, deep baking dishes should be used — with sides at least 6.5 cm (2½ inches) — so that the side of the dish can deflect the fanned heat away from the top surface. Trim the edges 2 cm (¾ inch) above the surface of the baklava, not evenly with the top of the dish as recommended. Another alternative is to place a piece of foil on top of the dish, shiny side down, and pressed firmly around edges. Pierce a few large holes in the foil for steam to escape. Leave on the baklava for the first 30 minutes while it is on the lower shelf, remove foil when repositioning dish on shelf above the centre of the oven. In this time the baklava should have dried out sufficiently to decrease the tendency for displacement. Use low fan speed if your oven has variable settings.

Round Pies and Tarts

Average commercially produced fillo sheets are 30 cm (12 inches) wide, just wide enough for a 23 cm (9 inch) pie dish. To prevent waste, cut fillo sheets into squares; you will be left with strips 15-20 cm (6-8 inches) wide — use for small pastries. Alternatively these strips can be placed side by side between the squares of fillo when buttering them. See Using Pastry Strips (page 70).

Round pie crusts Work with fillo sheets on flat surface for greater efficiency. Number of fillo squares used depends on thickness of sheets. Butter 6-8 fillo squares together using

Stack Method (page 69). Gently press into a greased pie dish, brush with butter, fill and top with a similar buttered stack. Press edges together and tuck corners and straight edges under, or trim off excess pastry with a Stanley knife or kitchen scissors.

An alternative method is as follows. Butter a fillo square, take next square and place at an angle so that corners are not together. Butter and place next sheet at a greater angle and continue in this manner, using 6-8 sheets altogether. Square will resemble a many-pointed star (with a little stretch of the imagination). This method gives an edge of more even width to tuck into sides of pie; as well, the fillo layers will more effectively enclose pies in deeper than average pie dishes.

Tart case or flan As these are one-crust pies, follow either of the methods for round pies and place buttered stack into greased pie or flan dish. Press gently into shape of dish and tuck edge in around rim, folding pastry over in soft folds. Do not press flat as the soft folds give a better effect. Brush top with butter and fit a piece of foil, shiny side down, into the crust. Add baking beans or rice and bake for 10 minutes at 180-190°C (350-375°F). Remove foil and beans and return to oven for 5 minutes or until golden.

Small tart cases Cut fillo sheets in half across the length to give rectangles, then cut these square. Size of square can be 20-25 cm (8-10 inches) depending on length of fillo sheet. Finish as for large cases, using buttered stack to line dishes up to 18 cm (7 inches) in diameter. Use 4 or 5 squares for small cases, and bake blind as above.

Using less fat Following the Book Method (page 70), every second sheet should be buttered or oiled. Butter first leaf, fold down two leaves, then butter the second. Again fold down two leaves and so on. If stack is to be cut into small squares after buttering, it is best to lightly butter every sheet, otherwise squares will be difficult to handle.

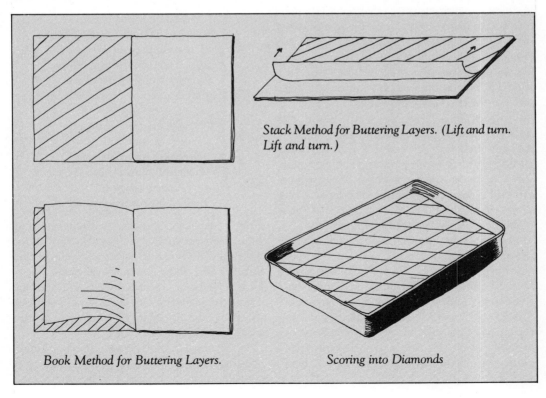

Stack Method for Buttering Layers. (Lift and turn. Lift and turn.)

Book Method for Buttering Layers.

Scoring into Diamonds

ZUCCHINI AND LEEK PIE

Serves 6 as a main course, 12 as a starter to a meal
Oven temperature
180-190°C (350-375°F)

500 g (1 lb) medium-sized zucchini
salt
3 cups chopped leeks (about 2 leeks)
⅓ cup olive oil
2 tablespoons grated romano or parmesan
cheese
1 cup crumbled feta cheese
2 tablespoons chopped parsley
4 eggs
½ cup sour cream
¼ teaspoon ground nutmeg
pinch cayenne pepper
freshly ground black pepper
24 sheets fillo pastry, see Buttering
Layers (page 69)
olive oil

Wash and trim zucchini and slice thinly. Place in colander, sprinkle on 1 tablespoon salt and toss well to distribute it. Leave for 30 minutes, rinse zucchini, drain and dry on a cloth. When preparing leeks, trim off most of the green top. Halve lengthwise and wash well between the leaves. Remove root end and chop, including some of the tender green leaves.

Put leeks in a frying pan with the oil and cook gently until just beginning to soften. Turn pan contents into a bowl and add the sliced zucchini, cheeses and parsley. Beat eggs with sour cream, nutmeg, cayenne, ½ teaspoon salt and a generous grinding of pepper. Pour onto vegetables and cheese and mix until well combined. Adjust seasoning if necessary.

Place half the fillo sheets in a stack and oil sheets following either of the two methods described. (To use less oil, follow Book Method, oiling every second sheet.) Place oiled stack into a lightly oiled baking or ovenproof dish 23 × 30 cm (9 × 12 inches) fitting it into the shape of the dish. Brush top of pastry with oil and cover dish with a slightly moistened cloth. Oil remaining fillo sheets. Cover these with a dry cloth.

Pour filling into pastry in dish and spread it evenly. Cover with the second stack of fillo and press the sides of the pastry together. Tuck in edges or, with a sharp knife or kitchen scissors, trim pastry level with top of dish. Brush top with oil. With a sharp knife score top 3 sheets of fillo in 3 or 4 evenly spaced lines running the length of the dish, according to the size of portions required. Sprinkle lightly with cold water and bake in a pre-heated moderate oven for 45 minutes. Let pie stand 10 minutes before cutting into squares to serve.

SPINACH PIE

Serves 6-12
Oven temperature
170-180°C (325-350°F)

1 bunch spinach, about 750 g (1½ lbs)
⅓ cup olive oil
1 small onion, chopped
1 cup chopped leek
½ cup chopped spring onion
¼ cup chopped parsley
2 teaspoons chopped fresh dill or
1 teaspoon dried dill tips
½ cup ricotta or cottage cheese
1 cup crumbled feta cheese
¼ cup grated romano or parmesan cheese
5 eggs
¼ teaspoon ground nutmeg
salt
freshly ground pepper
14-16 sheets fillo pastry, see Buttering
Layers (page 69)
melted butter or olive oil

Trim roots from spinach. Wash leaves and stalks well and drain thoroughly. Spread out on a large cloth and leave for 1-2 hours to dry. Shred leaves and stems fairly finely i.e. take a bundle of leaves, place on a board and cut across the leaves and stalks in 5 mm (¼ inch) shreds. Place in a flat dish and leave to dry further until required.

In a frying pan gently cook onion in oil until transparent, add leek and spring onion and cook gently for 5 minutes, stirring often. Leeks etc. should be transparent but still green. Remove from heat. Prepare chopped herbs.

In a large mixing bowl combine cheeses until well mixed. Beat in eggs, nutmeg, about ½ teaspoon salt and plenty of pepper. Fold in spinach, onion-oil mixture and herbs. Taste and add more salt if necessary.

Butter or oil fillo sheets together in 2 stacks, each stack with 7 or 8 sheets, depending on thickness. Cover one stack and place other stack in a greased 23 × 30 cm (9 × 12 inch) baking dish. Press gently into shape of dish, brush top with butter or oil and add spinach filling. Spread evenly and top with second stack of fillo. Press edges together and tuck in around sides of pie or trim evenly with rim of dish. Brush top with butter or oil. With a sharp knife, score top sheets lightly in 2 or 3 evenly spaced lines along the length of the dish.

Bake in a pre-heated moderate oven for 30 minutes below centre of oven and a further 30-40 minutes on shelf above centre of oven, so that pastry layers can cook evenly. Let pie stand for 10 minutes before cutting into squares to serve.

Note: Silverbeet (Swiss chard) may be used in place of spinach. Trim leaves from white ribs and keep ribs for another use. Wash, dry and shred leaves as for spinach. If using frozen leaf spinach, 2 250g (8oz) packs are required. Defrost, drain well pressing out moisture, and chop fairly finely. Add with onion-oil mixture.

BEAN AND VEGETABLE PIE

Serves 6-8
Oven temperature
180-190°C (350-375°F)

2 medium-sized eggplants
salt
2 tablespoons oil
1 large onion, sliced
1 clove garlic, crushed
½ green capsicum, cut in chunks
½ red capsicum, cut in chunks
2 cups diagonally sliced green beans
6 medium-sized zucchini, sliced thickly
425 g (15 oz) can peeled tomatoes,
chopped
2 tablespoons tomato paste
2 teaspoons chili powder (*see Note*)
2 tablespoons chopped parsley
300 g (10 oz) can red kidney beans
12-14 sheets fillo pastry, see Buttering
Layers (page 69)
melted butter or oil
1 tablespoon toasted sesame seeds

Cut eggplants into 2 cm (¾ inch) cubes with skin on. Place in colander and sprinkle well with salt. Toss well, then leave for 30 minutes. Rinse and drain, then spread onto absorbent paper to dry. Heat oil in a large pan, add onion and cook gently until transparent. Add garlic and eggplant and increase heat. Cook for 5 minutes, stirring often. Add capsicums, beans and zucchini and fry for a further 2 minutes. Reduce heat and add tomatoes, tomato paste, chili powder and parsley. Stir well, cover and simmer for 15 minutes. Add kidney beans and their liquid and simmer uncovered for 5 minutes. Keep aside — filling does not have to be cooled for this pie.

Butter and layer fillo sheets in 2 stacks as directed, using 6 or 7 sheets for each stack according to thickness of sheets. Grease a 23 × 33 cm (9 × 13 inch) ovenproof dish and line with one stack of fillo. Brush top with butter and spread vegetable filling in dish. Top with second buttered stack. Press edges of pastry together and fold in sides, or trim evenly with top of dish. Brush top with butter and sprinkle lightly with cold water if sides have been trimmed to prevent edges curling. Sprinkle on sesame seeds and bake in a moderately hot oven for 30 minutes until puffed and golden. Serve hot, cut into squares.

Note: Do not use the hot chili pepper in this recipe. Use the blended chili powder containing chili pepper, cummin, coriander and oregano; this chili powder is usually used for Chili Con Carne.

SPICED SPINACH AND POTATO PIE

Serves 4-5
Oven temperature
180-190°C (350-375°F)

500 g (1 lb) potatoes
1 medium-sized onion, chopped
2 tablespoons butter
1 clove garlic
½ teaspoon ground cummin
1 teaspoon ground coriander
¼ teaspoon chili powder, optional
1 teaspoon turmeric
250 g (8 oz) packet frozen leaf spinach,
thawed
1 tablespoon chopped fresh coriander
or mint
½ teaspoon garam masala
about 1 tablespoon lemon juice
salt
freshly ground black pepper
12-16 squares fillo pastry for Round Pie
Crust (page 70)
melted butter or substitute
¼ cup wheat germ

Peel and dice potatoes and boil until tender in salted water. Drain. In a frying pan cook onion in butter until transparent, add garlic, cummin, coriander, chili powder if used, and turmeric and cook gently for 3 minutes, stirring often. Roughly chop spinach, add to pan and stir over heat until most of moisture evaporates. Add cooked potatoes, coriander or mint, and garam masala. Mix lightly but thoroughly and add lemon juice, salt and pepper to taste. Keep aside.

Prepare fillo pie crusts as directed and sprinkle 2 teaspoons wheat germ on every second sheet. Place one crust into a greased 23 cm (9 inch) pie dish. Press gently into shape of dish, add filling and spread evenly. Top with second crust and tuck edges under. Brush top with butter and sprinkle with a little wheat germ. Bake in a moderately hot oven for 30 minutes until golden. Serve hot, cut in wedges, as a light meal.

GREEK CHEESE PIE

Serves 6 as a light meal, 12 as an appetiser
Oven temperature
180-190°C (350-375°F)

2 cups milk
½ cup fine semolina (cream of wheat)
2 tablespoons butter
1 cup coarsely grated Coon cheese
or other cheddar
1 cup crumbled feta cheese
¼ cup grated romano or parmesan cheese
4 eggs
¼ teaspoon ground nutmeg
¼ cup finely chopped parsley
salt
freshly ground pepper
12 sheets fillo pastry, see Buttering
Layers (page 69)
melted butter

In a heavy-based saucepan, combine milk and semolina, add butter and stir constantly over heat until thickened and bubbling. If sauce lumps, stir with a balloon whisk. Reduce heat and let mixture boil gently for 2 minutes. Add cheeses and stir until combined but do not overheat. Remove from heat and cool, stirring occasionally while cooling.

Beat eggs well and stir into cooled cheese sauce. Add nutmeg, parsley, and salt and pepper to taste.

Butter together 6 sheets fillo pastry, following Stack or Book method. Cover with a cloth. Butter together remaining sheets and cover. Grease a 23 × 30 cm (9 × 12 inch) baking dish and line with first stack of pastry. Pour in filling and spread evenly. Top with second lot of pastry. Brush top with butter and tuck pastry edges under to hold in filling. (Alternatively trim pastry level with rim of dish.) Lightly score top sheets in squares using a sharp knife. Avoid going through to filling if possible. Size of squares depends on number of serves required.

Sprinkle top lightly with cold water to prevent pastry curling and bake in a moderate oven for 40 minutes or until puffed and golden.

Cool in dish for 10 minutes. Cut into portions using scored lines as a guide and serve hot or warm. Serve with a tossed green salad, various greens, cucumber, green pepper, olives, chopped herbs, with a seasoned olive oil and vinegar dressing.

BACON AND EGG TARTS

Makes 6
Oven temperature
170-180°C (325-350°F)

As these tarts are excellent for a leisurely breakfast, preparation beforehand would save time and effort. Butter and stack fillo sheets, cut into squares and press into buttered muffin pans. Place pans in a large plastic bag and seal. Leave at room temperature overnight, fill and bake just before required for serving.

**125 g (4 oz) lean bacon
6 sheets fillo pastry, see Stack
Method (page 69)
melted butter or substitute
6 eggs
freshly ground pepper**

Remove rind from bacon if necessary. Chop bacon into small squares. Place in a greased, heated pan and cook until lightly browned. Drain on absorbent paper.

Butter the sheets of fillo together as directed. Cut into 6 12 cm (5 inch) squares and brush tops with butter. Lightly butter 6 large muffin pans. Insert squares of pastry, buttered side up, into each pan, moulding them into the shape of the pan, with corners standing up around the edges. Sprinkle some cooked bacon into each case. Carefully break an egg on top of the bacon and season lightly with pepper if desired.

Bake in a moderate oven for 12-15 minutes until pastry is golden and eggs are set (about 12 minutes for soft eggs, 15 minutes for hard). Serve hot for breakfast (one per serve) or with a salad for lunch (two per serve).
Note: A little sour or fresh cream may be spooned on top of each egg before baking.

CREAMED MUSHROOM TARTS

Serves 6
Oven temperature
180-190°C (350-375°F)

**12 sheets fillo pastry for Small Tart
Cases (page 71)
melted butter or substitute
500 g (1 lb) small fresh mushrooms
60 g (2 oz) butter
2 teaspoons lemon juice
3 spring onions, sliced diagonally
1 tablespoon chopped parsley
1 tablespoon chopped chives
½ teaspoon dried tarragon
½ cup cream
3 teaspoons cornflour
¼ cup white wine
½ cup sour cream
salt
freshly ground white pepper
chopped herbs or herb sprigs for garnish**

Stack fillo sheets and cut into 20 cm (8 inch) squares. Butter 4 squares together for each tart case and shape each case as directed, using greased 15-18 cm (6-7 inch) flan or pie dishes. Bake blind in a moderate oven for 15 minutes until crisp and golden. Remove tarts carefully from dishes and place on a greased baking sheet. These may be prepared ahead and warmed in a moderate oven for 7-8 minutes just before filling and serving.

Choose fresh plump cultivated mushrooms, flick any soil off with a dry cloth — do not wash. Trim stem and slice mushrooms thickly. Melt butter in a large frying pan until foaming, add mushrooms, sprinkle with lemon juice and stir over medium heat until just beginning to soften. Add spring onions, parsley, chives and tarragon. Stir in cream. Mix cornflour with white wine and stir into mushrooms. Keep stirring over heat until thickened and bubbling gently. Add sour cream and salt and pepper to taste. Heat through gently.

Place warm tart cases onto warmed serving plates and spoon hot filling into cases. Garnish with chopped herbs or herb sprigs and serve immediately as a first course.

MANGO SEAFOOD SHELLS

Serves 6
Oven temperature
180-190°C (350-375°F)

12 sheets fillo pastry for Small Tart
Cases (page 71)
melted butter or substitute
2 tablespoons desiccated coconut
250 g (8 oz) fresh scallops
½ cup dry white wine
12 medium-sized cooked prawns
12 large oysters (may be bottled oysters)
1 cooked lobster, about 500 g (1 lb)
or 3 crab sticks
1 large fresh mango or 425 g (15 oz) can
sliced mangoes
1 cup sour cream
2 tablespoons lemon juice
1 teaspoon ground ginger
½ teaspoon salt

Prepare and shape small tart cases as directed using fillo pastry and melted butter. When assembling fillo squares for the cases, sprinkle 1 tablespoon coconut on top of the second square of fillo before topping with the last 2 squares. Brush top with butter, insert foil and baking beans and bake in a moderately hot oven for 10 minutes, remove foil and beans and return to oven for further 5 minutes until golden. Leave to cool and remove from dishes. Cases may be prepared a day or two beforehand and stored carefully in a large sealed plastic container.

Clean any dark veins from scallops, leaving coral on scallops if present. Bring wine to a slow simmer, add scallops, let wine come back to simmering point, simmer 30 seconds only and remove pan from heat. Cool scallops in wine, then drain and refrigerate in a covered bowl.

Shell and devein prawns. Drain oysters. Take tail meat from lobster, remove dark vein and cut meat into 12 even-sized pieces. If using crab sticks, cut each stick into 4 pieces. Keep seafoods in covered separate bowls in refrigerator until required.

Cut fresh mango into 2 cm (¾ inch) cubes. If using canned mango, drain and cube slices.

Mix sour cream lightly with lemon juice, ground ginger and salt. Overmixing can cause sour cream to become too thick; if this occurs, stir in a little fresh thin cream. Mixture must be of a coating consistency.

To prepare for serving, place the fillo cases on small plates. Divide the various seafoods amongst the cases, piling them in the centre. Place mango cubes amongst seafoods. Spoon 2 tablespoons of the sour cream mixture over the seafoods and mango. Garnish plates as desired and serve cold as a starter.

CURRIED TUNA PIE

Serves 6
Oven temperature
180-190°C (350-375°F)

3 tablespoons butter
1 large onion, chopped
¼ cup chopped green capsicum
1 teaspoon grated fresh ginger
1 clove garlic, crushed
2 teaspoons curry powder
3 tablespoons flour
½ cup milk
½ cup cream
425 g (15 oz) can tuna chunks in brine
1 cup boiled rice
1 tablespoon lemon juice
12 sheets fillo pastry for Pie
Crusts (page 70)
melted butter or substitute
⅓ cup desiccated coconut, optional
Lemon Sauce for serving (page 31),
optional

Melt butter in a saucepan and add onion. Cook gently until transparent. Add capsicum, ginger, garlic and curry powder and cook for further 5 minutes. Stir in flour and cook 1 minute. Pour in milk and cream, stirring constantly until thickened and bubbling. Boil gently for 2 minutes and remove from heat.

Drain tuna thoroughly and flake with a fork, keeping pieces fairly large. Gently fold into sauce, add rice, salt and pepper to taste and lemon juice.

Make two pie crusts as directed using 6 sheets fillo pastry for each crust and sprinkling each second layer with 1 tablespoon coconut. Leave top of crusts unbuttered; cover one crust with a cloth. Grease a 23 cm (9 inch) square layer cake pan with butter and place one crust in pan, pressing it gently into shape of pan. Brush with butter and spread filling in pan. Butter second crust on one side and place buttered side down on top. Press crusts to seal. Trim corners and tuck edges around pie, or trim even with rim of pan, using a sharp knife or scissors. Brush top with melted butter and sprinkle with coconut. Bake in a moderately hot oven for 30 minutes until puffed and golden. Serve hot cut in squares and serve Lemon Sauce separately if desired.

GINGER SCALLOPS

Serves 6
Oven temperature
200-210°C (400-425°F)

375 g (12 oz) fresh scallops, with coral
if possible
¾ cup dry white wine
¼ teaspoon salt
2 tablespoons butter
1 clove garlic, finely chopped
2 tablespoons fine julienne of
fresh ginger
2 tablespoons flour
1 tablespoon dry sherry
1 teaspoon light soy sauce
freshly ground pepper
½ teaspoon sugar
3 spring onions
6 sheets fillo pastry
melted butter
mashed potato or boiled rice for holding
scallop shells

Clean dark veins from scallops, then rinse them. Bring wine to a gentle boil in a saucepan, add salt and scallops and let scallops poach gently for 30 seconds. Remove pan from heat, cover and leave for 5 minutes. Remove scallops from cooking liquid with a draining spoon and place in a bowl. Keep scallops and cooking liquid aside.

In a small pan melt butter, add garlic and ginger and sauté gently for 5 minutes. Sprinkle in flour, stir and cook gently for 2 minutes. Strain cooking liquid from scallops and add to pan, stirring constantly until sauce thickens and bubbles. Stir in sherry and soy sauce and a little more wine if sauce is too thick. Add pepper to taste, sugar and a little salt if necessary. Remove from heat and cover surface with plastic film to prevent skin forming. Clean spring onions and slice diagonally, including some of the green tops.

Butter together 4 of the fillo sheets. Cut the buttered stack into quarters. Butter together the 2 remaining sheets, cut in half, butter top of one half and place the other on top. Now cut this in half. You will end up with 6 buttered stacks of fillo about 15 cm (6 inches) wide and 20-25 (8-10 inches) long. Cover with a cloth. Take one stack and fold into 1 cm (½ inch) accordian pleats from the narrow end. Leave pleated while remaining fillo stacks are done.

Divide poached scallops between 6 large scallop shells (or small ovenproof dishes). Sprinkle spring onions on top and cover with sauce. Lightly brush the underside of a scallop shell with water and spread out pleated fillo on top. Gather pleats in at hinge end of scallop shell and fold fillo over the edge. Fan out the pleats and press edges onto the shell, allowing the pleats to be clearly defined. As each shell is covered, place on a 12-pan muffin or tart sheet so that rounded base of shell sits in one of the indentations (this keeps the shells straight during cooking). Brush pastry with butter and bake in a pre-heated hot oven for 10 minutes or until golden brown.

When serving, a little mashed potato or cooked rice on each plate will help keep the scallop shell in position. Garnish as desired and serve hot.
Note: After shells are filled and covered, place them on the muffin sheet, cover with foil and refrigerate until required. Put into the oven from the refrigerator and allow a little extra cooking time.

GREEK CHICKEN PIE

Serves 6-8
Oven temperature
170-180°C (325-350°F)

1 chicken, about 1.5 kg (3 lb)
3 cups water
1 carrot, quartered
1 small onion, quartered
1 small celery stalk, chopped
1 bay leaf
2 sprigs parsley
salt and pepper
⅓ cup butter
2 large onions, chopped
½ cup flour
½ cup milk
2 tablespoons grated romano or parmesan
cheese
4 eggs lightly beaten
¼ teaspoon ground nutmeg
16 sheets fillo pastry, see Buttering
Layers (page 69)
melted butter
1 tablespoon toasted sesame seeds,
optional

Rinse chicken and place in a large pot with water, carrot, onion, celery, bay leaf and parsley. Add about 2 teaspoons salt and pepper to taste. Bring to a slow simmer, skimming when necessary, cover and simmer gently for 1 hour until chicken is tender. Remove chicken from pot and separate flesh from bones and skin. Return bones and skin to pot and boil, uncovered, for 30 minutes. Dice chicken flesh, place in a large bowl and cover. Strain chicken stock into a measuring jug and make up to 2 cups with water if necessary.

Melt butter in a clean heavy pan and add chopped onion. Cook gently until transparent. Sprinkle flour over onions, stir and cook for 2 minutes. Pour in chicken stock and stir constantly until thickened, add milk and stir until bubbling. Add sauce to chicken in bowl. Stir in cheese and nutmeg. Cool to lukewarm and mix in lightly beaten eggs. Adjust seasoning.

Butter fillo sheets in two stacks of 8 sheets each as directed. Keep 1 stack covered with cloth. Line a greased 23 × 30 cm (9 × 12 inch)

baking dish with a stack of fillo, brush with butter. Spread filling in dish and cover with second stack of fillo, press edges together and fold in sides. Brush top with butter. With a sharp knife score through 3 top sheets along length of dish in 2 vertical lines, evenly spaced. Sprinkle sesame seeds on top if desired.

Bake in a moderate oven for 45 minutes until puffed and golden. Let pie stand for 10 minutes before cutting into squares to serve.

MOUSSAKA PIE

Serves 6-8
Oven temperature
180-190°C (350-375°F)

2 large oval eggplants
salt
oil for frying eggplant
1 large onion, chopped
2 tablespoons oil or butter
1 clove garlic, crushed
750 g (1½ lbs) coarsely ground beef
¼ cup tomato paste
½ cup red wine
freshly ground black pepper
¼ teaspoon ground cinnamon
1 teaspoon sugar
2 tablespoons chopped parsley
2 eggs
1 cup sour cream
pinch ground nutmeg
12 sheets fillo pastry, see Buttering
Layers (page 69)
melted butter or substitute

Cut eggplants into 5 mm (¼ inch) slices with skin on. Spread out onto a tray and sprinkle well with salt. Leave for 30 minutes, then rinse and dry with absorbent paper. Heat about ¼ cup oil in a frying pan and fry eggplant slices until lightly browned on each side. Remove and drain on absorbent paper. Add more oil as required to the pan to fry all the slices. Alternatively brush eggplant slices with oil and place in an oiled baking dish. Cook under a hot grill until browned on each side. This latter method results in eggplant which is a lot less oily. Keep aside.

Cook onion in oil until soft, add garlic and ground meat and increase heat. Stir often to break up lumps and cook until meat changes colour. Reduce heat, add tomato paste, red wine, salt and pepper to taste, cinnamon, sugar and parsley. Cover and simmer gently for 20 minutes. Beat eggs in a bowl and beat in sour cream and nutmeg. Keep aside with the meat mixture.

Butter the fillo sheets and form into 2 stacks of 6 sheets each. Cover one stack with a cloth and place second stack of fillo in a greased 23 × 30 cm (9 × 12 inch) ovenproof or baking dish. Gently ease fillo stack into shape of dish and brush top of fillo with butter.

Place a layer of browned eggplant slices on the fillo and spread meat mixture on top. Pour sour cream and egg mixture evenly over the meat and top with remaining eggplant slices. Place remaining fillo stack on top and press edges of pastry together. Trim evenly with rim of dish. Brush top with butter and score lightly through top sheets into squares. Sprinkle lightly with cold water and bake in a moderately hot oven for 45 minutes or until puffed and golden. Let pie stand for 10 minutes before cutting into squares to serve. A tossed Greek style salad is all the accompaniment required.

GREEK MEAT PIE

Serves 6-8 as a main meal
Oven temperature
170-180°C (325-350°F)

1 large onion chopped
2 tablespoons butter
750 g (1½ lbs) finely ground beef
1 clove garlic, crushed
½ cup water
2 tablespoons tomato paste
½ teaspoon sugar
salt
freshly ground pepper
⅛ teaspoon cinnamon
¼ cup chopped parsley

⅓-½ cup grated romano or parmesan cheese
3 eggs, lightly beaten
24 sheets fillo pastry, see Buttering Layers (page 69)
melted butter or substitute

In a large frying pan cook onion gently in butter until transparent. Add ground meat and garlic, increase heat and cook, stirring well to break up lumps, until meat changes colour. Reduce heat, add water, tomato paste, sugar, about 1 teaspoon salt, a good grinding of black pepper and the cinnamon. Cover and simmer gently for 15 minutes or until only a little moisture remains. Remove to a bowl and cool. Stir in parsley, cheese to taste and eggs.

Butter half of the fillo pastry sheets together following the Stack or Book method and brush top sheet with butter. Place in a greased 23 × 30 cm (9 × 12 inch) baking or ovenproof dish. Cover dish with a lightly moistened cloth. Butter remaining sheets together, cover and keep aside.

Put filling into lined dish and place stack of buttered sheets on top. Fold pastry in around sides of pie or cut level with top of dish using a knife or scissors, and brush top with butter. With a sharp knife score top 3 sheets of pastry in 2 or 3 lines along the length of the pie, spacing them evenly.

Sprinkle top lightly with water and bake in a moderate oven for 45 minutes. Let pie stand for 10 minutes before cutting into serving portions.
Note: To use less fat, follow the Book Method and butter every second sheet.

BAKLAVA

Makes 30 pieces
Oven temperature
160°C (325°F)

Number of sheets used depends on size and thickness of sheets in a 375 g (12 oz) pack. Measure size of sheets against dish, allow for sides of dish and cut off excess. These may then be placed between whole sheets when buttering them. See Using Pastry Strips (page 70).

2 cups chopped walnuts
2 cups chopped almonds
¼ cup caster sugar
2 teaspoons ground cinnamon
⅛ teaspoon ground cloves
24-30 sheets fillo pastry, see Buttering
Layers (page 69)
¾ cup melted butter
SYRUP:
1½ cups sugar
1½ cups water
¼ cup honey
thinly peeled strip of lemon rind
small piece cinnamon stick
3 cloves
2 teaspoons lemon juice

Chop nuts in food processor with steel blade, preparing walnuts and almonds separately. Mix with sugar, cinnamon and cloves.

Butter base and sides of a 23 × 30 cm (9 × 12 inch) baking dish. Put 2 sheets fillo aside and cover. Divide remaining sheets in 2 stacks and butter each stack as directed, using any off-cuts between layers. Place one stack in dish and brush top with melted butter. Spread half of the nut mixture over fillo. Top with reserved two sheets of fillo brushing each with butter. Spread remaining nuts on fillo and top with remaining fillo stack. Press edges of fillo together and trim edges level with rim of dish. Brush top with butter.

Cut baklava with a sharp knife into diamond shapes (see directions page 70). Sprinkle lightly with water to prevent top layers curling upwards. Bake on centre shelf in a moderately slow oven for 30 minutes. Move up one shelf and cook for further 45 minutes. Cover with greased brown paper if top colours too quickly.

Pastry must be allowed to cook through.

When baklava goes into the oven, make the syrup. Place sugar, water and honey in a heavy pan and stir occasionally over medium heat until sugar is dissolved. Add remaining syrup ingredients, bring to the boil and continue to boil for 15 minutes. Do not stir while boiling but skim when necessary. Strain and cool.

When baklava is cooked, spoon cold syrup evenly over hot pastry. Leave for several hours before cutting again into serving portions. Store baklava in a sealed container at room temperature.

LEBANESE ALMOND BAKLAVA

Makes about 40 pieces
Oven temperature
170-180°C (325-350°F)

SYRUP:
2 cups sugar
1½ cups water
2 teaspoons lemon juice
2 teaspoons rose water
ALMOND FILLING:
1 egg white
1 cup caster sugar
3 cups coarsely ground almonds
2 teaspons orange flower water
2 drops almond essence
TO FINISH:
36-40 sheets fillo pastry, see Buttering
Layers (page 69)
1 cup melted butter
½ cup chopped pistachio nuts, optional

Make syrup first. Place sugar and water in a heavy pan, stir over medium heat until dissolved and add lemon juice. Bring to the boil and boil for 15 minutes over medium heat. Do not stir syrup after it begins to boil. Stir in rose water, remove from heat and leave aside to cool. Syrup should be of thin honey consistency when cool.

To prepare filling, in a bowl beat egg white until stiff and gradually beat in sugar. Fold in almonds, orange flower water and almond essence. Keep aside.

Divide fillo pastry into 2 equal stacks; number of sheets required depends on thickness of fillo. Cover one stack with dry then damp cloths. Butter other stack as described for Stack or Book method. Brush a 23 × 30 cm (9 × 12 inch) baking dish with butter and place stack of fillo pastry in dish. Brush top with butter. Spread nut filling evenly onto fillo. Cover with a cloth. Butter remaining stack of fillo sheets and place on top of nut filling. Press sides of pastry together and trim edges with a sharp knife.

Brush top with butter and cut through fillo layers in diamond shapes (see illustration, page 71). Pour any remaining butter evenly over pastry. Sprinkle top lightly with cold water. Bake on centre shelf in a moderate oven for 30 minutes; raise one shelf above centre and cook for further 30-40 minutes, but do not allow pastry to become too brown.

Pour cooled syrup over hot pastry and leave until cold. Sprinkle with pistachio nuts if desired. Cut through pastry again and lift pieces out carefully with a spatula. Store in a sealed container at room temperature, not in refrigerator.

PETALED NUT PASTRIES

Makes about 40
Oven temperature
170-180°C (325-350°F)

These pastries are made in Greece, Syria, Lebanon and Turkey. The Greek pastries are sometimes called Aginares *meaning artichokes; in Lebanon they are sometimes known as* Baklawa Be'Aj, *after the kerchief-wrapped bundle in which belongings are carried. But usually they are just called* Baklava *or* Baklawa, *depending on the language of the region.*

The Greek version is flavoured with cinnamon and lemon, while Arabic pastries are fragrant with rose and orange flower water.

SYRUP:
2 cups sugar
1½ cups water
strip of lemon rind
2 teaspoons lemon juice
small cinnamon stick

NUT FILLING:
2 egg whites
½ cup caster sugar
2 cups coarsely ground walnuts
2 cups coarsely ground almonds
1½ teaspoons ground cinnamon

TO FINISH:
24-30 sheets fillo pastry, see Buttering Layers (page 69)
1 cup melted butter

To make the syrup, dissolve sugar in water over heat, add lemon rind and juice and cinnamon stick and bring to the boil. Boil on medium heat for 20 minutes and do not stir while boiling. Strain into a jug and leave aside to cool.

To prepare the filling, in a bowl beat egg whites until stiff and beat sugar in gradually. Fold in nuts and ground cinnamon. Keep aside.

Stack 8-10 sheets fillo pastry (depending on thickness) on a flat surface. Keep remainder covered with a dry, then a damp cloth. Butter sheets together following Stack or Book Method. Leave top and bottom of stack unbuttered. With kitchen scissors cut buttered stack of fillo into approximately 8 cm (3 inch) squares.

Butter top of fillo square and place a tablespoonful of nut mixture in the centre. Gently squeeze into a lily shape, with four corners of square as petals and filling in centre. Place filled pastries close together in a buttered 25 × 33 cm (10 × 13 inch) baking dish. Butter another 2 stacks of fillo, cut into squares, fill and shape. Prepare one lot at a time as butter can harden if left too long, and pastries are then difficult to shape. When all are completed, brush pastries with remaining butter.

Bake in a moderate oven for 45 minutes, until golden. When cooked, remove from oven and pour cool thick syrup over hot pastries. Leave until cool before serving. Store in a sealed container at room temperature.

COPENHAGEN TORTE

Makes about 30 pieces
Oven temperature
180-190°C (350-375°F)

While the name might suggest that this is a Danish torte, it is in fact a Greek torte known as Kopenhai. It was created to commemorate the investiture of a Danish prince as King George I of Greece.

PASTRY BASE:
¾ cup butter
¼ cup caster sugar
grated rind of 1 orange
2 egg yolks
1½ cups plain flour
pinch salt

ALMOND SPONGE FILLING:
6 eggs, separated
½ cup caster sugar
¼ teaspoon almond essence
½ cup plain flour
½ teaspoon baking powder
2 cups ground almonds
pinch salt

TO FINISH:
8 sheets fillo pastry, see Buttering
Layers (page 69)
melted butter
2 cups sugar
1 cup water
thin strip lemon rind
2 teaspoons lemon juice
large piece cinnamon stick

Cream butter and sugar in a mixing bowl, adding orange rind, and beat until light and fluffy. Beat in egg yolks. Sift flour and salt and fold into butter mixture. Mix to a soft dough and knead lightly until smooth. Cover with plastic film and rest for 15 minutes. Roll out on a lightly floured board and place in a greased 25 × 30cm (10 ×12 inch) baking dish. Press into shape of dish, covering base and sides. Pastry moulds easily, so any tears can be pressed together. Trim pastry level with top of dish. Bake in a moderate oven for 20 minutes until lightly coloured, remove and leave until cool.

While pastry is baking, make almond filling. Beat egg yolks with sugar and almond essence until thick and light. Sift flour with baking powder and mix into the ground almonds. Fold this mixture lightly into the egg yolks, using a metal spoon.

Beat egg whites with salt until stiff and fold lightly into almond mixture. Pour into pastry in dish and smooth with a spatula.

Butter fillo sheets together following Stack or Book method. Leave top of stack unbuttered. Place on top of the almond filling and trim edges of fillo in line with pastry crust, using scissors or a sharp knife.

Brush top with butter and score top sheets lightly in lines running the length of the dish, spacing them 4 cm (1½ inches) apart. Bake in a moderate oven for 45 minutes until top is golden and cake is cooked — test with a fine skewer.

While torte is baking, make a syrup. Place sugar and water in a heavy pan and stir occasionally over gentle heat until sugar is dissolved. Add lemon rind, juice and cinnamon stick and bring to the boil. Boil, without stirring, for 10 minutes, strain into a jug and leave until cool.

When torte is cooked, cut through slits in pastry down to the bottom crust. Spoon syrup over torte, leave until cool, then cut diagonally into diamonds for serving. Store any left over torte in a sealed container at room temperature.

Note: While not traditional, whipped cream may be served as an accompaniment to tone down the sweetness of the torte. With strawberries, it can serve as an interesting dessert, particularly if catering for a crowd.

KATAIFI

Even experienced cooks are mystified when they first encounter kataifi pastry. (It is pronounced with evenly stressed syllables: ka-ta-if-ee; the first syllable, as in 'cut'.) It looks like vermicelli when fresh and resembles shredded wheat breakfast cereal when cooked. While its uses so far have been for sweet, syrup soaked pastries, it can also be used for savoury goods.

Kataifi is made with a batter using gluten-free flour. The smooth batter is poured through a container peppered with fine holes. The fine streams of batter fall onto a revolving heated metal plate where they are cooked briefly, then scooped off while still pliable. Kataifi is marketed as *Kataifi*, the Greek name for this pastry; in Arabic countries it is known as *Konafa* (also as *Konafeh, Kunafeh* and *K'nafi,* depending on the dialect of the region, which alters the transliteration). In Turkey it is known as *Kadaif.*

Fillo pastry makers also make kataifi and, while a few supermarkets stock it along with fillo, it is generally available only from Greek, Middle Eastern and Armenian delicatessens and food stores. It is packaged in a sealed plastic bag in a cardboard box; the details on the pack are adequate if you are familiar with the product. It has a life of 2 months or so in the refrigerator, providing the plastic package is sealed well. In the freezer it will keep for 6-8 months. As Kataifi transports well, you can stock up on it whenever you find supplies.

HANDLING KATAIFI

While it is not as temperamental as fillo pastry, for certain recipes kataifi requires a little dexterity when rolling it up. As kataifi does not absorb butter in the same way as fillo does, most recipes give butter quantities as excess butter is wasteful.

Remove kataifi from refrigerator 3-4 hours before required (remove from freezer 8 hours beforehand), to allow strands to soften. With kataifi still in the sealed plastic pack, knead with hands for a minute or so. This makes the kataifi springy, and strands are easier to spread or separate. Remove required amount from pack to a bowl, reseal pack and return to refrigerator.

Melt and clarify butter as directed on page 10. As a general rule, use ½ cup melted butter (125 g or 4 oz) for 250 g (8 oz) kataifi. Pour butter over kataifi and mix through the strands with fingers. Alternatively, kataifi can be placed in a baking utensil and melted butter dabbed onto kataifi with a brush. Recipes expand on preparation techniques.

CHOW MEIN KATAIFI

How is that for a mixture of cultures! Kataifi makers never dreamed their product could be used for chow mein noodles, but indeed it can be.

To make traditional chow mein noodles, egg noodles have to be boiled, drained, spread out to dry for a while, then dropped into hot oil and fried until crisp — with much spitting, spluttering and fuming. Kataifi pastry eliminates all of this, as the frying is both brief and spatter, splutter and fume-free.

Naturally with something which has such advantages, there might be a disadvantage and fried kataifi has its limitations. Let moist food sit on it for too long and it softens — not too much of a disadvantage really. I recommend that the fried kataifi be placed around the edge of the serving platter with the stir-fried meat and vegetables placed in the centre. Additional fried kataifi can be served in a separate bowl. A word of warning. Kataifi cannot be boiled like noodles — its ingredients are such that it dissolves when boiled.

Fried Kataifi Heat oil for deep frying until very hot. Take a handful of kataifi and drop into oil. Fry a few seconds, turn with frying spoon and fry for another few seconds until golden brown. Kataifi sizzles only briefly in the oil, then continues to cook without any obvious activity. When fried remove with frying spoon onto crumpled absorbent paper and drop another handful into the oil. 125 g (4 oz) kataifi is sufficient for the average meal. Place some of the lightly crumbled crisp kataifi around the edge of the serving platter and pile the cooked meat and vegetables in the centre. Serve remaining kataifi separately in a bowl.

Toasted Kataifi Chow Mein without the added calories! Instead of frying the kataifi, spread the strands on a baking sheet and place in a moderate oven for 15 minutes. Turn the clump of strands half way through baking to brown more evenly. If you like, a little peanut oil may be dabbed onto the kataifi with a brush before baking. Serve as for fried kataifi.

BREAKFAST KATAIFI

Oven temperature
180-190°C (350-375°F)

You can make these breakfast rolls with left-over uncooked kataifi, or use a pack of kataifi if you have the patience.

Squeeze kataifi in the hands to loosen the strands. Take a small amount of strands (about the size of a walnut when squeezed) and spread it out on a board so that strands roughly run away from you. Roll up tightly, squeezing strands together as you roll. Finished pastry should be like a small cocktail sausage. Place rolls close together in a lightly greased slab cake pan. If you like, you can dab the tops of the rolls lightly with butter or polyunsaturated oil, or leave them plain. Bake in a moderately hot oven, one shelf above centre, for 20-25 minutes until golden brown and crisp. Cool in pan and store in a sealed container.

To serve, place a few rolls in a cereal bowl, add some chopped nuts (pecans, walnuts, almonds etc), dried fruit such as sultanas, raisins, prunes, apricots, peaches (chopped where necessary), grated fresh apple, or whatever takes your fancy. Add wheatgerm, sweetening in the form of honey or a sugar and a little cold milk or cream. Do not add too much liquid as the crunchy texture will be lost. A delicious breakfast — yes, almost like shredded wheat cereal!

These rolls will keep for 2 weeks or so if butter or oil is added when baking, a month or more if cooked without fat.

Right: *Kataifi Nests (page 90); Hazelnut Chocolate Tarts (page 91) and Fruit Cream Tarts (page 92).*
Overleaf: *A selection of traditional fillo and kataifi pastries. From top row, left to right — Semolina Cream Rolls (page 43); Pistachio Kataifi (page 93); Nut Triangles (page 24); Shirred Almond Rolls (page 25); Kataifi Nut Rolls (page 91); Petaled Nut Pastries (page 81); Lebanese Almond Baklava (page 80); Rolled Baklava (page 63); Sultan's Turbans (page 26) and Shirred Almond Rings (page 25).*

EGG CROUSTADES

Serves 4
Oven temperature
180-190°C (350-375°F)

125 g (4 oz) kataifi for Nests (page 90)
melted butter
3 tablespoons firm butter
1 cup sliced small mushrooms
1 teaspoon lemon juice
½ cup diced ham
6 eggs
freshly ground pepper
4 tablespoons cream
salt
1 tablespoon chopped chives

Squeeze kataifi to loosen strands and place in 8 buttered brioche moulds or large muffin pans. Press into shape of pans, with kataifi covering sides and base. Use a glass tumbler to compact the kataifi. Dab with melted butter and bake in a moderate oven for 15-20 minutes. Remove cases to a baking sheet and keep warm.

Melt 1 tablespoon butter in a frying pan and add mushrooms and lemon juice. Sauté a few minutes then add ham and cook a little longer. Leave on a low heat.

Beat eggs lightly with a fork, mix in pepper and cream. (Do not overbeat eggs.) Melt remaining butter in a heavy heated pan and heat until foaming, but do not allow it to colour. Stir a pinch of salt into the eggs and pour into pan. Allow them to set slightly then stir gently but constantly with a wooden spoon until eggs are creamy and moist. Remove from heat and gently fold in ham and mushroom mixture. Pile into warm kataifi cases and sprinkle tops with chives. Serve immediately, 2 per serve.
Note: Any of your favourite scrambled egg variations may be served in this way.

Bean and Vegetable Pie (page 73) and Creamy Spinach Coils (page 30).

THATCHED BEEF PIE

Serves 6
Oven temperature
170-180°C (325-350°F)

1 kg (2 lb) chuck steak
¼ cup flour seasoned with salt
and pepper
2 tablespoons butter or oil
3 medium-sized onions, sliced
½ teaspoon dried thyme
1 cup tomato purée
½ cup water
1 beef stock cube
2 teaspoons Worcestershire sauce
125 g (4 oz) kataifi pastry
melted butter

Trim beef, cut into 3 cm (1¼ inch) cubes and coat with seasoned flour. Heat half the butter in a frying pan and brown meat cubes quickly, adding a single layer to the pan at a time. Add more butter if necessary. Remove to a deep pie or casserole dish.

Add more butter to pan if necessary with the onions and gently fry onions until transparent. Sprinkle on any remaining flour and stir over heat for 1 minute. Add thyme, tomato purée, water, crumbled stock cube and sauce and stir until thickened and bubbling. Pour over beef and mix well. Do not add more liquid as meat juices will add to liquid content during cooking. Cover dish with lid or foil and cook in a moderate oven for 2 hours or until beef is tender.

Meanwhile knead kataifi in your hands to loosen strands. Place on a greased baking sheet and shape into size to fit top of dish. Bake in the oven for 15-20 minutes until golden.

To serve, remove cover from pie dish or casserole and clean rim. Place kataifi on top of the meat. Crumble edges of kataifi if necessary so that it fits into dish. Garnish if desired and take to the table.
Note: This is a simple, but good-tasting beef casserole. Any meat or chicken casserole can be finished in this way. While you might be tempted to place the uncooked kataifi on top of the meat casserole to cook, strands will melt into the sauce during cooking, leaving very little kataifi to crisp and brown.

BEEF CHOW MEIN

Serves 5-6

500 g (1 lb) round steak
½ teaspoon bicarbonate of soda
1 teaspoon soy sauce
2 teaspoons dry sherry
2 tablespoons peanut oil
2 small onions, quartered and
leaves separated
½ cup diagonally sliced celery
1 cup green and red capsicum strips
1 cup diagonally sliced green beans
1 cup sliced mushrooms
1 teaspoon grated fresh ginger
1 clove garlic, crushed
additional tablespoon soy sauce
additional 2 tablespoons sherry
2 teaspoons sugar
½ cup beef stock
2 teaspoons cornflour
125 g (4 oz) kataifi pastry, see Fried
Kataifi (page 84)

Trim meat and cut into long, thin strips. Place
in a bowl with soda, soy sauce and sherry. Mix
thoroughly and leave for 30 minutes.

Heat half the oil in a wok or large frying pan
and add onion, celery, capsicum and beans.
Stir-fry for 3-4 minutes, add mushrooms and
stir-fry for a further minute. Remove vegetables to a bowl and keep aside. Add remaining
oil to wok, heat well and add ginger, garlic and
beef strips. Stir-fry on high heat until meat is
just cooked through — do not overcook. Return
vegetables to wok and toss over medium heat
for a minute.

Blend additional soy sauce with sherry, sugar,
stock and cornflour. Pour into wok contents
and stir over heat until thickened and beginning to bubble. Serve in the centre of a serving
platter with fried kataifi around edge, and
remainder of fried kataifi in a separate bowl.
Boiled rice may accompany the meal.

KATAIFI BASKETS
OR NESTS

Edible baskets made from potatoes or noodles
have long been used by chefs for attractive
presentation of foods, but they require time
and skill to prepare. Kataifi pastry can create a
similar effect with a lot less fuss.

While kataifi may be inserted between 2
strainers and deep fried (in a manner similar to
noodle and potato baskets), it is much easier to
prepare kataifi baskets in the oven, without the
exorbitant calories of fried food.

Their size and shape depends on your needs.
Little nests (for example for holding quail eggs
as a garnish for quail) may be shaped in small
rounded tart pans. Large muffin pans or brioche
moulds may be used for making small baskets or
tart cases. Oval deep pie dishes or casseroles
are suitable for shaping an oval basket for food
presentation while round casseroles and cake
pans may shape round baskets and loaf pans
and terrine moulds rectangular shapes. The
size and shape of kataifi baskets are limited only
by your imagination and cookware.

To make baskets or nests Kataifi should be at
room temperature. Squeeze kataifi pastry while
in its plastic bag to loosen strands. Remove
amount required — a little nest requires a very
small handful, while large shapes could take
half a pack or more. Grease the utensil with
butter, put kataifi into utensil and press into
shape. Use a pad of absorbent paper to press
little nests; the base of a small glass tumbler to
press kataifi into muffin pans; sides and base of
a glass tumbler to press kataifi into shape in
large utensils.

Using melted, clarified butter, dab kataifi
lightly with a brush dipped in the butter. You
can use as little butter as you like, or none at all
if you prefer, but do not saturate the kataifi as it
absorbs little butter.

Bake shapes in a moderate oven until golden
brown and crisp. Time depends on size of shape.
With deeper shapes the inside is usually pale —
if it is allowed to colour, the rest of the shape
will overcook.

Shapes should be used hot from the oven,
removed from utensil and placed on serving
plate.

They can be prepared beforehand, or used cold, or reheated in a moderate oven on an oven slide. Store cooked shapes in an airtight container. Fill shapes just before serving with hot or cold food. Do not fill, leave aside and heat with the food in the shape, as the kataifi may soften.

Meanwhile dissolve sugar in water over heat, add lemon juice and rind, cloves and cinnamon. Bring to the boil and boil over medium heat without stirring for 10 minutes. Stir in honey, boil 1 minute, strain and cool.

Pour cooled syrup over hot pastries and place folded paper towels on top to allow steam to slightly soften pastries. Leave until cool and store in a sealed container at room temperature.

KATAIFI NUT ROLLS

Makes about 30 rolls
Oven temperature
170-180°C (325-350°F)

375 g (12 oz) kataifi pastry
¾ cup melted butter
NUT FILLING:
1 cup coarsely ground walnuts or pecans
1 cup coarsely ground almonds
½ cup caster sugar
1 teaspoon ground cinnamon
¼ teaspoon ground cloves
1 egg white, lightly beaten
1 tablespoon brandy
SYRUP:
2 cups sugar
1½ cups water
1 teaspoon lemon juice
thin strip of lemon rind
4 cloves
small piece cinnamon stick
1 tablespoon honey

Knead kataifi. Take a small handful of the pastry strands and spread out fairly compactly on a board in a small rectangle with strands roughly running towards you. Size of rectangle should be about 6 cm (2½ inches) wide and 15 cm (6 inches) long. Using a pastry brush, dab some melted butter over the strands.

Combine nut filling ingredients and mix to a coarse paste. Shape a tablespoon of filling into a short sausage shape and place along narrow edge of pastry. Roll up firmly into a neat roll. Squeeze roll gently in the hand to firm it. Repeat with remaining ingredients. Place rolls in a buttered baking dish, spacing them a little apart. Brush tops with remaining butter. Bake in a moderate oven, one shelf above centre, for 50-55 minutes until golden brown.

HAZELNUT CHOCOLATE TARTS

Makes 18
Oven temperature
170-180°C (325-350°F)

250 g (8 oz) kataifi pastry
½ cup melted butter
90 g (3 oz) dark chocolate, melted
HAZELNUT CREAM FILLING:
1¼ cups milk
2 tablespoons cornflour
¼ cup sugar
2 egg yolks
pinch salt
1 teaspoon vanilla essence
½ cup ground toasted hazelnuts
½ cup thickened cream, whipped
FOR SERVING:
whipped, lightly sweetened cream
whole toasted hazelnuts or chocolate
curls to decorate

Put loosened kataifi strands in a bowl. Pour melted butter over kataifi and mix through strands with finger tips. Place small handfuls of kataifi into large muffin pans. Mould kataifi into shape of pans using fingers and use a straight-sided small glass tumbler to firm the pastry strands. Bake in a moderate oven for 15-20 minutes until lightly browned on top and sides; inside of tarts will still be pale. Cool in pans and remove to a wire rack.

When cold, spread a thin layer of melted chocolate on the inside of each case. To do this more easily, scoop melted chocolate so that it coats the back of a teaspoon and spread into cases.   (continued overleaf)

To make filling, mix milk, cornflour, sugar, egg yolks and salt in a heavy based saucepan. Stir over medium heat with a wooden spoon until thickened and bubbling gently. Stir in vanilla essence and hazelnuts and remove from heat. Press a piece of plastic film over the surface of the custard and leave until cool. Remove film and stir custard to smooth it. Fold in whipped cream. Put generous tablespoons of hazelnut custard into prepared chocolate coated cases in soft mounds.

Pipe or spoon a swirl of whipped cream in the centre of each tart and decorate with a whole hazelnut or with chocolate curls.

Fruit Cream Tarts Follow directions for making chocolate coated tart cases in above recipe. Make custard as directed, replacing vanilla with 1 tablespoon kirsch and omitting hazelnuts. Cool, fold in cream and spoon into chocolate cases. Arrange whole or halved strawberries, well drained apricot halves, sliced kiwifruit, whole fresh raspberries or blueberries on top of custard. Brush fruit with warm, melted, red currant jelly preserve or sieved apricot jam to give a glaze.

CUSTARD KATAIFI ELENI

Serves 12
Oven temperature
170-180°C (325-350°F)

SYRUP:
¾ cup water
1 cup sugar
thin strip of lemon rind
small piece cinnamon stick
2 teaspoons lemon juice
KATAIFI CRUST:
125 g (4 oz) kataifi pastry
½ cup melted butter
TOPPING:
2 cups milk
¼ cup cornflour
2 eggs, beaten
pinch salt
¼ cup sugar

1 teaspoon vanilla essence
1 tablespoon brandy, optional
1 cup cream, whipped
1 tablespoon caster sugar
½ teaspoon vanilla essence
½ cup toasted flaked or slivered almonds

To make the syrup, place water and sugar in a small, heavy pan and heat, stirring occasionally, until sugar is dissolved. Bring to the boil; add lemon rind, cinnamon stick and lemon juice and boil, without stirring, for 12 minutes. Strain into a jug and leave to cool.

Knead kataifi in its plastic bag until loose and remove required amount to a bowl. Pour on melted butter and mix with fingers to distribute butter evenly. Press into the base of a 19 × 30 cm (7½ × 12 inch) ovenproof dish. A straight-sided glass tumbler rolled over pastry helps to compact it. Bake in a moderately hot oven for 20-25 minutes until golden — do not let kataifi become too brown. Remove from oven and pour cold syrup evenly over the hot kataifi. Cover dish with a cloth so that steam can slightly soften kataifi. Leave to cool completely.

Combine milk and cornflour in a heavy saucepan. Beat eggs with salt and sugar and stir into milk. Place pan on medium heat and stir constantly until custard thickens and bubbles. Let custard boil gently for 1 minute. Stir in vanilla essence and brandy if used and remove from heat. Cool for 10 minutes, stirring occasionally to prevent skin forming, then pour while still hot onto the kataifi. Cool completely and cover dish with plastic film. Chill for 1 hour.

Whip cream until stiff and fold in caster sugar and vanilla essence. Spread over custard and sprinkle toasted almonds evenly on top. Serve cut in squares as a dessert.

PISTACHIO KATAIFI

Makes 30 pieces
Oven temperature
170-180°C (325-350°F)

Pistachios are the most expensive of the nuts, but you can extend them with blanched almonds and still retain the colour contrast with the kataifi. Unfortunately there is a tendency for nut processors to salt pistachios. As the nuts have to be blanched, the salt is effectively removed in the process.
To blanch pistachios, place shelled nuts in a bowl and pour on boiling water. Leave for 5 minutes or until skin can be removed easily. Drain and skin. Spread on a tray and dry out in a slow oven for 5 minutes.

SYRUP:
1 cup water
1½ cups sugar
1 teaspoon lemon juice
1 teaspoon rose water
1 teaspoon orange flower water
PISTACHIO FILLING:
1½ cups finely chopped blanched
pistachio nuts (or use a mixture
of pistachios and blanched almonds)
1 egg white
¼ cup caster sugar
½ teaspoon rose water
½ teaspoon orange flower water
TO FINISH:
375 g (12 oz) kataifi pastry

¾ cup melted butter

To make the syrup, place water and sugar in a heavy pan and dissolve over medium heat, stirring occasionally. Add lemon juice and bring to the boil. Boil on medium heat for 15 minutes. Add rose and orange flower water, boil 1 minute, remove from heat and leave to cool.

Nuts for the filling may be prepared in food processor using steel blade. Process just long enough to chop fairly finely. Beat egg white until stiff and beat in sugar. Fold in nuts, rose and orange flower water.

Squeeze kataifi while in its plastic bag to loosen strands. Take a sixth of the kataifi and spread out on a board to an 18 × 25 cm (7 × 10 inch) rectangle with strands running roughly away from you. Dip brush in melted butter and dab butter over the strands. Place about 3 tablespoons nut filling along one narrow edge. Roll up firmly into a neat roll. Make 5 more rolls with the kataifi and filling.

Place rolls a little apart in an 18 × 28 cm (7 × 11 inch) slab cake pan or baking dish. Brush remaining butter on top of rolls. Bake in a moderate oven, one shelf above centre, for 50-55 minutes until golden and crisp.

When cooked, pour cold syrup over the hot rolls. Cover with folded absorbent paper and leave until cool. When cold and syrup has been absorbed, cut each roll diagonally into 5 pieces. Store in a sealed container at room temperature.

USING THE RECIPES
Measures

Both metric and imperial measures are given for the weight of ingredients; however the majority of ingredients are given in cup, graduated cup and spoon measures as it is a more efficient way to cook.

If following metric weights, use the 250 ml cup measure, 20 ml tablespoon and 5 ml teaspoon. For imperial weights, use the 8 fl oz cup measure, ½ fl oz tablespoon (15 ml), and ⅛ fl oz teaspoon (5 ml). Dry ingredients should be levelled in graduated cup or spoon measures.

Fillo pastry quantities have been given in number of sheets rather than by weight. See Fillo Statistics (page 7) for approximate number of sheets to a pack.

Oven Temperatures

Gas and electric ovens vary, and two temperatures are given for the majority of recipes. Follow the lower temperature for gas ovens, the higher temperature for electric. Only one temperature is given in some instances when a slow oven heat is required, as there is little difference between the two types of ovens lower down the temperature scale. Temperatures are given in both degrees Celsius (Centigrade) and degrees Fahrenheit.

GLOSSARY OF INGREDIENTS

Some ingredients are known by different names in some areas, while other ingredients may not be familiar to some cooks. The following glossary will clarify certain ingredients used in the recipes.

Capsicum: Sweet bell pepper — may be green or red.

Caster sugar: Fine, granulated sugar or superfine sugar.

Cornflour: Cornstarch.

Fillet: Tenderloin. Relates to pork as well as beef.

Fillet – short: The thick end of the whole fillet (tenderloin) usually weighing 750-900 g (1½-2 lb). This is the fillet usually available from the butcher and it can be cut into fillet steaks. It comprises two muscles, one tapering into the other.

Icing sugar: Confectioners' or powdered sugar.

Orange flower water: A fragrant liquid distilled from orange blossoms, it is available at Greek and Middle Eastern food stores. Chemists (druggists) sell a concentrated essence, and if this is the only one available, use a drop at a time to flavour the syrup or nut filling until a pleasant fragrance is just discernible. Take care when using the essence.

Rose water: Distilled from fragrant rose petals and available from the same outlets as orange flower water. Again take care if only the essence is available.

Sausage mince: The ground meat mixture used for making fresh link sausages. If unavailable without the casing, use link sausages and remove the casing.

Silverbeet: Swiss chard.

Spring onions: Also known as green onions, scallions and shallots. The latter is incorrect as a shallot is shaped like a large, elongated garlic clove and, when dried, has a brownish skin. A small bulbous white onion with green tops (leaves) is also a spring onion, however its leaves are coarse and cannot be used as can the leaves of the slender spring onion.

Index

Page numbers in *italics* denote photographs and illustrations.

Adding the fat   9
Advance preparation of pastries   28
Almond flutes   25
Almond rings, shirred   25, 86
Almond rolls, shirred   25, 86
Amandine, seafood   46, 54
Appetisers/Snacks
  Bacon and onion triangles   23
  Brain tricorns   16
  Cheese straws   17, 23
  Cheese triangles   15
  Chinese chicken and crab rolls, *see* Chinese chicken and ham rolls
  Corn puffs   16
  Crab and pecan bites   22
  Curry puffs   20
  Fried camembert triangles   17, 24
  Fried wontons   18, 21
  Ladies' fingers   17, 22
  Little spinach triangles   17, 15
  Samosa with meat filling   19
  Samosa with vegetable filling   19
  Sausage rolls   23
  Seafood fillo rolls   17, 20
  Spring rolls   41
Apple coils   49
Apple strudel   60
Apricot lamb in fillo   35, 42
Apricot nut veal, *see* Veal cordon bleu
Apricot puff   62
Avocado puffs, chicken and   36, 38
Avocado, tarragon fish with   34

Background to fillo pastry   6
Bacon and egg tarts   75
Bacon and onion triangles   23
Bagged carpetbag steaks   41, 66
Baklava   80
  Lebanese almond   80, 86
  rolled   63, 86
Banana date roll   62
Bananas calypso   43
Basic shaping of pastries
  coils   27, 29
  parcel I   28, 29
  parcel II   28, 29
  rolls (small)   14, *14*
  roll I   27
  roll II   27, *29*
  triangles (large)   27
  triangles (small)   13, *14*
Baskets or nests, kataifi   85, 90
Bean and vegetable pie   73, 88
Bechamel sauce   32
Beef
  chow mein   90
  cobbler   56
  pie, thatched   89
  stilton   40
  Wellington   56, 66
Bird's nest pastries   49
Bird's nest pastries with fruit   48, 49
Blintzes, smoked salmon   31, 46
Book method (buttering layers)   70, *71*
Bougatsa, *see* Semolina cream rolls
Boureks, cheese, *see* Cheese triangles
Boureks, spinach, *see* Little spinach triangles
Braid, plum strudel   61, 65
Brain and spinach triangles   30
Brain tricorns   16

Brush, the   11
Butter   10
  and oil   10
  clarified or drawn   10
  melted, a short cut   10
  quantities   10
  substitutes   10
Buttering layers of fillo sheets   69, 71
Buying and storing fillo pastry   6
Calypso, bananas   43
Calypso sauce   44
Camembert triangles, fried   17, 24
Caribbean, pineapple   44
Carpetbag steaks, bagged   41, 66
Cheese
  boureks, *see* Cheese triangles
  pie, Greek   74
  sauce   53
  straws   17, 23
  strudel   64
  strudel, cherry   60
  triangles   15
Cherry cheese strudel   60
Chicken
  and avocado puffs   36, 38
  and broccoli roll   55
  and crab rolls, Chinese, *18*, 37
  and ham rolls, Chinese   *18*, 37
  pie, Greek   78
  rolls, mango   38
Chinese chicken and crab rolls, *see* Chinese chicken and ham rolls
Chinese chicken and ham rolls   *18*, 37
Chocolate fingers, hazelnut   26
Chocolate tarts, hazelnut   85, 91
Chili sauce   21
Chilled fillo   7, 8
Chow mein, beef   90
Chow mein kataifi   84
Cinnamon sticks   24
Clarified margarine   10
Clarified or drawn butter   10
Cobbler, beef   56
Coconut sticks, *see* cinnamon sticks
Coils, apple   49
Coils, creamy spinach   30, 88
Coils, shaping   27, 29
Convection ovens, *see* Fan-forced ovens and fillo
Cookware and fillo   11
Copenhagen torte   82
Corn puffs   16
Crab and pecan bites   22
Creamed mushroom tarts   68, 75
Creamy spinach coils   30, 88
Curried tuna pie   76
Curry puffs   20
Custard kataifi Eleni   92
Cutting and scoring into diamonds   70, 71
Cutting fillo   8

Date roll, banana   62
Date wontons   26
Decorating the big wrap   51
Desserts
  Apple coils   49
  Apple strudel   60
  Apricot puffs   62
  Banana date roll   62
  Bananas calypso   43
  Bird's nest pastries   49
  Bird's nest pastries with fruit   49, *49*
  Cheese strudel   64
  Cherry cheese strudel   60
  Copenhagen torte   82

  Custard kataifi Eleni   92
  Dried fruit strudel   64
  Fried camembert triangles   17, 24
  Peaches 'n cream   45, 50
  Pineapple Caribbean   44
  Plum strudel braid   61, 65
  Semolina cream rolls   43, 86
  Walnut strudel   59
Drawn butter, clarified or   10
Dried fruit strudel   64

Egg and cheese dishes
  bacon and egg tarts   75
  cheese straws   17, 23
  cheese triangles   15
  egg croustades   89
  fried camembert triangles   17, 24
  Greek cheese pie   74
Egg croustades   89
Enlarged fillo wrap   51

Fan-forced ovens and fillo   70
Fat, adding the   9
Fat, using less   11
  on bigger wrap-ups   28
  on little wrap-ups   14
  on pies and tarts   71
Fish, fried filloed   33
Fish with avocado, tarragon   34
Fish, *see* Seafood dishes
Flan, tart case or   71
Folding or cutting fillo sheets   12
Freezer storage of prepared pastries   11
Freezer, to cook pastries from the   11
Fried camembert triangles   17, 24
Fried kataifi, *see* Chow mein kataifi
Fried filloed fish   33
Fried wontons   18, 21
Frozen fillo   7, 8
Fruit cream tarts   85, 91-92

Ghee   10
Ginger scallops   46, 77
Greek cheese pie   74
Greek chicken pie   78
Greek meat pie   79

Ham and asparagus rolls with egg sauce   42
Handling fillo   8
Home-made fillo pastry   12
Hazelnut chocolate fingers   26
Hazelnut chocolate tarts   85, 91

Kataifi
  baskets or nests   85, 90
  breakfast   84
  chow mein   84
  custard Eleni   92
  fried, *see* Chow mein
  nut rolls   86, 91
  pistachio   86, 93
  toasted, *see* Chow mein
Koulibiaka   54

Ladies' fingers   17, 22
Lamb in fillo, apricot   35, 42
Lamb loin en croute   57
Lamb loin with cherry stuffing   58
Lebanese almond baklava   80, 86
Leek pie, zucchini and   72
Lemon sauce   31
Little spinach triangles   15, *17*

Mango chicken rolls   38
Mango seafood shells   76

Margarine, clarified 10
Meat dishes
  Apricot lamb in fillo 35, 42
  Bagged carpetbag steaks 41, 66
  Beef chow mein 90
  Beef cobbler 56
  Beef stilton 40
  Beef Wellington 56, 66
  Curry puffs 20
  Fried wontons 18, 21
  Greek meat pie 79
  Ladies' fingers 17, 22
  Lamb loin en croute 57
  Lamb loin with cherry stuffing 58
  Moussaka pie 78
  Pork Glen Huon 58
  Pruned pork packets 40
  Samosa with meat filling 19
  Sausage rolls 23
  Spring rolls 41
  Thatched beef pie 89
  Veal cordon bleu 39
Melted butter 10
Microwave oven, fillo and the 8
Moussaka pie 78
Mousseline of seafood Evans 32

Nantua sauce 32
Nut pastries, petaled 81, 86
Nut rolls, kataifi 86, 91
Nut triangles 24, 86

Oil 10
Oil and butter 10

Panada, see Corn puffs
Parcel I, shaping 28, 29
Parcel II, shaping 28, 29
Pastries, advance preparation of 28
Pastries, bird's nest 49
Pastries, freezer storage of prepared 11
Pastries, petaled nut 81, 86
Pastry strips, using 70
Peaches 'n cream 45, 50
Pie crusts, round 70
Pies and tarts, round (shaping) 70
Pineapple Caribbean 44
Pistachio kataifi 86, 93
Plum sauce 17, 22
Plum strudel braid 61, 65
Poppy seed strudel 63
Pork Glen Huon 58
Pork packets, pruned 40
Prawns Piraeus 34, 46
Prepared pastries, freezer storage of 11
Prepared pastries, to cook from
    freezer 11
Preparing strips 13
Problems, fillo 9
Pruned pork packets 40

Quantities, butter 10
Quiche, note on 69

Resurrecting fillo pastry 9
Rolled baklava 63, 86
Rolls for baking (small) 14
Rolls for frying (small) 14
Roll I, shaping 27
Roll II, shaping 27, 29
Round pie crusts 71
Round pies and tarts 70

Sabayon sauce 45, 50
Salmon blintzes, smoked 31, 46
Samosa with meat filling 19
Samosa with vegetable filling 19

Sauce
  bechamel 32
  calypso 44
  cheese 53
  chili 21
  lemon 31
  nantua 32
  plum 17, 22
  sabayon 45, 50
  yoghurt 20
Sauces, serving 28
Sausage rolls 23
Scallops, ginger 46, 77
Seafood amandine 46, 54
Seafood dishes
  Crab and pecan bites 22
  Fried filloed fish 33
  Fried wontons 18, 21
  Ginger scallops 46, 77
  Koulibiaka 54
  Mango seafood shells 76
  Mousseline of seafood Evans 32
  Prawns Piraeus 34, 46
  Seafood amandine 46, 54
  Seafood fillo rolls 17, 20
  Smoked salmon blintzes 31, 46
  Smoked trout with horseradish
      cream sauce 33
  Tarragon fish with avocado 34
Seafood fillo rolls 17, 20
Semolina cream rolls 43, 86
Serving sauces 28
Silverbeet 94
Small tart cases 71
Smoked salmon blintzes 31, 46
Smoked trout with horseradish cream
    sauce 33
Snacks, see Appetisers
Spiced spinach and potato pie 74
Spinach
  and potato pie, spiced 74
  boureks, see Little spinach triangles
  coils, creamy 30, 88
  pie 72
  triangles, brain and 30
  triangles, little 15, 17
Spring rolls 41
Stack method (buttering layers) 69,
    71
Starters
  Brain and spinach triangles 30
  Creamed mushroom tarts 68, 75
  Creamy spinach coils 30, 88
  Ginger scallops 46, 77
  Greek cheese pie 74
  Ham and asparagus rolls with egg
      sauce 42
  Mango seafood shells 76
  Mousseline of seafood Evans 32
  Prawns Piraeus 34, 46
  Seafood amandine 46, 54
  Smoked salmon blintzes 31, 46
  Smoked trout with horseradish cream
      sauce 33
  Spinach pie 72
  Zucchini and leek pie 72
Statistics, fillo 7
Steaks, bagged carpetbag 41, 66
Sticks, cinnamon 24
Sticks, coconut, see Cinnamon sticks
Storing fillo pastry, buying and 6
Strudels, about 52
Sultan's turbans 25-26, 86
Sweet pastries
  Almond flutes 25, 86
  Apricot puff 62
  Baklava 80

Bird's nest pastries 49
Cheese strudel 64
Cinnamon sticks 24
Coconut sticks, see Cinnamon sticks
Copenhagen torte 82
Dried fruit strudel 64
Fruit cream tarts, see Hazelnut
    chocolate tarts
Hazelnut chocolate fingers 26
Hazelnut chocolate tarts 85, 91
Kataifi nut rolls 86, 91
Lebanese almond baklava 80, 86
Nut triangles 24, 86
Pistachio kataifi 86, 93
Poppy seed strudel 63
Rolled baklava 63, 86
Semolina cream rolls 43, 86
Shirred almond rings 25, 86
Shirred almond rolls 25, 86
Sultan's turbans 25, 86
Walnut strudel 59

Tarragon fish with avocado 34
Tart case or flan 71
Tart cases, small 71
Tarts
  bacon and egg 75
  creamed mushroom 68, 75
  hazelnut chocolate 85, 91
  mango seafood shells 76
Toasted kataifi, see Chow mein kataifi
Triangles
  Bacon and onion 23
  Brain and spinach 30
  Cheese 15
  for baking (small) 13
  for frying (small) 13
  Fried camembert 17, 24
  Nut 24, 86
  Shaping large 27
  Shaping small 13, 14
Tricorns, brain 16
Trout, smoked with horseradish cream
    sauce 33
Tuna pie, curried 76

Unused fillo, handling 8
Using less fat, see Fat
Using pastry strips 70

Veal, apricot nut, see Veal cordon bleu
Veal, camembert, see Veal cordon bleu
Veal cordon bleu 39
Veal, mozzarella, tomato and basil,
    see Veal cordon bleu
Vegetable dishes
  Bean and vegetable pie 73, 88
  Creamed mushroom tarts 68, 75
  Creamy spinach coils 30, 88
  Little spinach triangles 15, 17
  Samosa with vegetable filling 19
  Spiced spinach and potato pie 74
  Spinach pie 72
  Spinach triangles, brain and 30
  Vegetarian delight 53
  Zucchini and leek pie 72
Vegetable filling, samosa with 19
Vegetarian delight 53

Walnut strudel 59
Wellington, beef 56, 66
Wontons, fried 18, 21
Working with fillo 7
Wrap, enlarged fillo 51

Yoghurt sauce 20

Zucchini and leek pie 72